IN QUEST OF CABELL

IN QUEST OF CABELL

Five Exploratory Essays

by

WILLIAM LEIGH GODSHALK

THE JAMES BRANCH CABELL SERIES

REVISIONIST PRESS
New York
1975

First printing April 1975. This edition is limited to 200 copies.
Copyright © 1975 by William L. Godshalk. All rights reserved.

THE REVISIONIST PRESS
G.P.O. Box 2009
Brooklyn, N.Y. 11202

Library of Congress Catalog Card Number: 74-50
International Standard Book Number: 0-87700-217-7

Printed and Bound in the United States of America

To Anne Godshalk,
    Lauri Godshalk,
    and Elihu and Heather

Preface

In the twenties, James Branch Cabell was the preeminent American writer. His European critics cited his work as evidence that American letters had at last come of age, and many American commentators were just as adulatory in their praise. Even a hostile critic, Peter Monro Jack, called the 1920's "The James Branch Cabell Period." Nevertheless, in the United States, Cabell's novels were as widely deprecated as they were appreciated. He was generally considered to verge on the pornographic; some thought his style to be turgid and effete; others frowned upon his political and social attitudes. Cabell became the whipping boy of the school of criticism which welcomed Hemingway on the one hand and the New Deal on the other. His art was never thoroughly understood, and the myths he was creating about man's life in an alien universe were passed over in search for more salacious matter. Thus, after a decade of acclaim, Cabell was gradually forgotten, and his writing disappeared from both the popular and the learned anthologies. As he himself noted in one of his last autobiographical pieces, his books were seldom, if ever, read. A specious type of liberalism had, for the moment, triumphed. During the past few years, however, the tides of taste have begun to change, and Cabell is again being recognized by discriminating readers for what he is: one of the masters of American fiction.

    The son of Dr. and Mrs. Robert Gamble Cabell, II, James was born in Richmond, Virginia, on April 14, 1879. Through both parents, he was related to the best families of Virginia. In his first years was fostered the love of myth and fable which distinguished much of his writing. One of his favorite books as a child was Charles Henry Watson's <u>Stories of the Days of King Arthur</u>. Perhaps equally important in the growth of his artistic temperament were the embellished reminiscences of the Civil War which permeated the Richmond atmosphere of his youth. As he grew older, he became fully aware of the discrepancy between this cozy world of myth and the actual world in which both the Arthurian and the Southern heroes lived.

    My own interest in Cabell began as a consequence of my exploration of Joseph Conrad's ironic use of Christian myth in <u>The Heart of Darkness</u>. In 1965, on leave from the College of William and Mary, I held a post-doctoral fellowship at the University of North Carolina, Chapel Hill. After discussing my ideas of the ironic use of myth with Anne McFarlane (who later became my wife), she said, "You should read Cabell's <u>The Silver Stallion</u>. It's an ironic description of a Christ-like myth." "Who's Cabell?" I asked, and she told me. Upon my return to William and Mary, I began to study Cabell's work and to explore his college career. The hierarchy of William and Mary, however, was not very happy with my investigation. There had been some scandal involving Cabell during his last year at the college, and scandals are always to be forgotten and surely never to be investigated. However, with the encouragement of Cabell's wife, Margaret Freeman Cabell, I persevered, and the result is the first essay in this volume. Something did happen during Cabell's senior year, and at least one boy left college because of the mysterious incident. But at the very most, Cabell must have been only peripherally involved.

The second essay of this volume appeared originally as the Introduction to an edition of <u>Beyond Life</u>. My friend and colleague at William and Mary, Scott Donaldson, asked me to write the essay, and although it is specifically concerned with <u>Beyond Life</u>, it generally explores the growth of Cabell's style and esthetic credo.

Cabell's sources have intrigued literary detectives since the twenties. Unfortunately, most of the source-hunters have been little more than finger-pointers. "Hey look," they shout to us, "Cabell read this book and he took such-and-such a name and such-and-such an incident from it." My answer is usually, "So what?" And my third essay is a brief attempt to indicate the proper method of discussing source material. The source-hunter should not only point to a source; he should also suggest why and how the author uses the source.

"Cabell's _Cream of the Jest_ and Recent American Fiction" grew out of a seminar at the Modern Language Association Meeting in 1970. The topic of the seminar was Cabell's relationship to modern fiction, and after listening to the discussion, I decided that _The Cream of the Jest_ would be a good place to begin an exploration of Cabell's influence on later novelists. I sent my completed essay to Louis Rubin, one of the editors of _The Southern Literary Journal_ (in which the essay was first published). A few weeks later, Louis called me on the telephone and commissioned the final essay in this volume for a book of essays he was editing, _The Comic Imagination in American Literature_, for Rutgers University Press. He asked me to explore more fully my ideas about Barth's relation to Cabell, and so this last essay has all the marks of a sequel. I think I make quite a good case for Barth's familiarity with Cabell's writing, but I should, in all fairness to the reader, record Barth's own comment: "I know J. B. Cabell's works only at second hand; have never been curious enough, despite several critics' comparisons, to know them at first. So . . ." Like Jurgen, I feel that the facts are at times intolerable. It is completely unfair that my pleasant intellectual structure should be toppled by a mere shred of evidence, and so the final essay stands as it is. Though Mr. Barth may never have read Cabell, I prove beyond question that their kinship rises above familiarity.

These five essays, then, are episodes in my personal quest for an understanding of Cabell: Cabell the man, Cabell the artist, and Cabell the historical portent.

Acknowledgements

The material in Chapter 1 first appeared in *William and Mary Review*, 5, No. 2 (1967), 1-10; the material in Chapter 2, in *Beyond Life* published by the Johnson Reprint Corporation; the material in Chapter 3, in *Kalki*, 6 (1974), 63-67 published by the James Branch Cabell Society; the material in Chapter 4, in *The Southern Literary Journal*, 5 (1973), 18-31; and the material in Chapter 5, in *The Comic Imagination in American Literature*, edited by Louis Rubin and published by Rutgers University Press. The Selected Bibliography was first in the Johnson edition of *Beyond Life*. The essays and bibliography are reprinted, with minor changes, by permission of the editors and presses involved.

Table of Contents

Chapter 1: James Branch Cabell at William and
           Mary: The Education of a Novelist 1

Chapter 2: The Growth of a Credo: Beyond Life. 20

Chapter 3: Cabell's Sources: The Mirror of
           Illusion and Reality. 47

Chapter 4: Cabell's Cream of the Jest and
           Recent American Fiction 55

Chapter 5: Cabell and Barth: Our Comic Athletes. 76

Selected Bibliography. 90

Chapter 1: James Branch Cabell at
William and Mary: The Education
of a Novelist[1]

In the 1920's, James Branch Cabell was one of the best known contemporary authors. From 1904 to 1930, he published twenty-nine books, one of which, Jurgen, gained notoriety as a result of an unsuccessful attempt to suppress it in New York because of its supposed indecencies. In general, Cabell's novels were well received; and Carl Van Doren, H. L. Mencken, and Warren McNeill between 1927 and 1932 published full-length studies of the Cabellian artistry. Much like Eliot's Wasteland, Cabell's novels are replete with learned allusions, and in the late 20's James Cover and John Phillips Cranwell provided explanatory notes to Jurgen and Figures of Earth--suggesting a wide public interest. During the period, Cabell was a regular and distinguished contributor to the Smart Set, and the short story which grew into Jurgen first appeared in its pages. Among the literary men of the time, Cabell's circle of friends was large: Sinclair Lewis, Joseph Hergesheimer, Carl Van Vechten, Burton Rascoe, Arthur Machen, to name a few. In his Nobel Prize Address in 1930, Lewis mentioned Cabell as one of the three American writers, along with Hemingway and Faulkner, worthy of the attention of the Swedish Academy. All in all, Cabell's reputation in the 20's must have seemed unassailable. But fortune's wheel turned, and the years that followed his initial popularity gave rise to a series of hostile critics.

Cabell's novels were attacked from almost every conceivable position: stylistically, ideologically, socially, personally. In 1933, Granville Hicks, abdicating the critic's responsibility of balanced judgment, strikes at the author himself, calling him "a sleek, smug egoist," and his work "a structure of lies." Hicks begins the series of attacks; and Oscar Cargill in Intellectual America (1941), after damning "Cabell's reputation as a stylist" as "overblown," attempts to have the final word. He sums Cabell up "as a museum piece representing the psychology of a Virginian who would be an intellectual leader yet had not quite what it takes."

However, the 1950's had better words for Cabell. Edward Wagenknecht in the Cavalcade of the American Novel (1952) reminds us that "James Branch Cabell . . . is still a unique and incomparable figure in American literature. . . . He will never be the voice of a 'party' or of a 'movement'; he will never speak for anything smaller or more limited than the human spirit itself." Four years later, Edmund Wilson in a long article in the New Yorker suggested that Cabell's work had been maligned by partial critics and called for a reevaluation of his novels. In the 60's two book-length studies have appeared, and a biography is in preparation. Joe Lee Davis concludes that "one must--in common decency and simple justice--rank him among the major rather than the minor authors of the twentieth century. . . . Cabell is both the Spenser and the Boccaccio of the second American Renaissance."[2] After years of neglect, Cabell's work is again receiving the attention it deserves.

His major achievement is the series of eighteen novels he called "The Biography of the Life of Manuel." Technically written in the romantic form and the comic mode, the novels trace the lineage of Count Manuel from a mythical French province of Poictesme to Lichfield, Virginia. Although Cabell with tongue in cheek suggested that his volumes were to be read "simply" as stories "for pastime" wherein "neither morality nor symbolism is . . . educed,"[3] the romances indeed form a symbolic commentary on the human situation. Torn between the ideal and the real, Cabellian man is forever thwarted in his quest for the ideal by the demands of the real. Cabell explores all the aspects of this human dilemma, perhaps reaching the conclusion that man can never achieve his ideals, simply because he must exist in the world of reality; and yet, for his self-preservation in that world he must, paradoxically, cling to these very ideals, unrealized, unrealizable. Even in the face of materialistic denial of spiritual value, man must believe in some kind of transcendent worth.

Although the meaning of Cabellian comedy can be comprehended without the ability to recognize each learned allusion, the incidents of the novels are often based on classical, Russian, Hebrew, medieval, and even Aztec myths and legends. The reader is quite obviously in the presence of a learned author, and many of Cabell's intellectual pursuits can be traced to his college years. In 1894, at the age of fifteen, James Branch Cabell entered the College of William and Mary.

When Cabell came to Williamsburg in the fall of that year, the College was small, with 160 students, all men, and by the end of Cabell's four-year stay, the enrollment had increased by only thirty. The complexion of the College was provincial, with most of the students from within the state, and a very few from the surrounding areas, Washington or West Virginia. Many of the students were from rural backgrounds, and Cabell is said to have stood out in his city dress, yellow gloves and cane. According to the records, a majority of the students was planning to become teachers, and Cabell was one of forty who did not list his intention to enter the profession. The faculty included only seven professors (called by the students "the Seven Wise Men," perhaps in half-jest), each teaching one or more of the disciplines of study. Professor John Lesslie Hall, for example, taught both English and history. Three or four instructors or assistants, often drawn from former graduates or even from the student body, filled out the faculty.

The small library with its very high shelves was open only during certain hours, and Charles W. Coleman, who had gained a name as a "Virginia poet," was the librarian whose duty it was to direct the reading of the students. Cabell and those students of literary taste and ability were drawn to Coleman, "the poet in residence," and Cabell later said that Coleman along with Professor Bishop had introduced him to classical, medieval French and Provençal literature, all lasting influences on his later work. To friends, Cabell confided that Coleman was the prototype of his fictional character "Charteris," who in <u>Beyond Life</u> lives in the small town of "Fairhaven" with an eighteenth-century background and a small college. Young Cabell was doubly fortunate, for he was boarding with Mrs. Cynthia Beverley Tucker Coleman, with whom, Charles Coleman, her son, lived also. The College had few dormitories, and most students lived in certain approved boarding houses in the town. Mrs. Coleman taught one of the Bible classes at Bruton Parish Church, at which young Cabell sang in the choir.

On Campus, several fraternities were active, including PBK, and Cabell belonged to Alpha Sigma Alpha which merged with Kappa Alpha in 1896. We may conjecture that Cabell was quickly forgiven his city manners and dress. Dances were held, and young ladies attended. Professor Bird, the youthful teacher of Pedagogy, and his wife were often present and mingled freely with the students. Public lectures and debates were sponsored, though the students were perhaps more interested in the "pretty frocks" present from town than the actual words of the speakers. In 1896, Charles Coleman gave an informal talk to Professor Hall's English Club on contemporary literature. "The authors of which he spoke were principally Southern writers," says the report in the <u>William and Mary College Monthly</u> (V, 221). Coleman illustrated his talk with photos and autographs. On the other hand, when Jones's Pond froze in the winter, most of the students went skating. Life at the College had many aspects.

Sports were also played on the intercollegiate level. At one point in Cabell's senior year, as the baseball season was approaching, the student Athletic Association felt that the team lacked a suitable pitcher and so petitioned the faculty to allow one to be searched out and enrolled in the College--without attending classes--that he might legitimately play for the William and Mary team. Denouncing the concept of "professionalism" in college sports, the faculty denied the request. A few months before, during the football season, one of the College players had been expelled for appearing on the field with "dirty words" written in black ink on his jersey. His request to return was denied, perhaps because he had also broken down the door of his room and had been guilty of other disorderly conduct. Obviously, the "Virginia gentlemen" were at times less than the code demanded, and life at the College was a little more racy than the College Catalogue would have led parents to believe. One can hardly think that Cabell felt extremely repressed by the stultifying social atmosphere of a conservative Virginia college.

At the same time, it has been suggested that Cabell was, at William and Mary, inhibited intellectually rather than socially, and thus turned to his teachers and advisors for mental companionship. Although this may indeed have been the case, with our present store of facts it seems impossible adequately to determine. We can observe, however, that Cabell did not neglect his studies, and each year saw him gain several Certificates of Distinction: his freshman year in Greek and French; his sophomore year in English, Greek, and French; his junior year in English, mathematics, Latin, Greek, and German; his senior year in "Moral Science, Political Economy, and Civil Government" and in history. We have record of Cabell's taking courses and distinguishing himself in every area of study offered at William and Mary except "Natural Science" and "Pedagogy." The diversity of his studies suggests the width of both Cabell's interests and his abilities, which, in turn, are reflected in his later writings. However, as his Certificates of Distinction and his later novels indicate, Cabell's forte was languages, and his most influential professor, Charles Edward Bishop, who helped introduce him to the glories of ancient Greece and medieval France.

With his doctorate from Leipzig, Professor Bishop taught Greek, French, and German. In an editorial in the

Monthly (V, 66-67) the student editor complained that Bishop was vastly overworked by the College, having little time for his own scholarship; he was lecturing more than 20 hours a week. Many of Bishop's methods and aims of teaching language may now seem outdated; but one of his major aims, "to read the great thoughts, aspirations, dreams, threats, longings of the great intellects of the world" (Monthly, VI, 275-279), helps us to understand his influence on Cabell. In personal appearance Bishop was a small man, wearing a pointed beard and glasses. During his junior year, Cabell became Bishop's assistant; and although no written record of this relationship appears to be extant, we may conjecture that it was mutually profitable, and that Cabell gained an increased knowledge of Greek and French, his favorite subjects. It was Bishop who introduced Cabell to C. C. Fauriel's History of Provençal Poetry.

In his senior year, Cabell finally mustered the fortitude to take the "Junior Class" of President Tyler's "Moral Science, Political Economy, and Civil Government," which in the 1897-98 session concentrated on Moral Science: logic, ethics, history of philosophy. Tyler was an arch-conservative, fighting to preserve an age which was passing. How did Cabell react to his teaching? Did he rebel against his conservative views? At this point in his intellectual life, Cabell's views, as we shall see in his contributions in the

Monthly, tended toward liberalism. Did Cabell perhaps agree with some of Tyler's tenets? Later in *Jurgen*, he viciously satirizes the evils of popular democracy. It is impossible to define their relationship, but we do know that when Cabell needed serious advice, he consulted President Lyon G. Tyler.

Cabell also took courses under Professor John Lesslie Hall and achieved distinction. A publishing scholar, Hall's orientation was philological, emphasizing Anglo-Saxon and the history of the language. Indeed, *Jurgen's* "Master Philologist" blinking "through his great spectacles" (Hall wore glasses) may owe something to Professor Hall. But Hall provided young Cabell with more than a hint for a character in a later novel, and perhaps a distaste for philological scholarship. As an advanced student in English, Cabell would have studied Shakespeare under Hall, who organized a special "Shakespeare class" early in 1896. Though the standards were high, the course was popular--"the most agreeable and fascinating of all the studies that our College affords" (*Monthly*, V, 159). In Cabell's later fiction, the influence of Shakespeare is recurrent, and Joe Lee Davis claims that "it can . . . be demonstrated . . . that Cabell had a Shakespeare obsession" (p. 55). It is possible to trace that love of Shakespeare to Cabell's course under Professor Hall. In the Catalogue, Hall reminded his students that "essays suitable for the College magazine are required at stated intervals."

Cabell was active on the staff of the William and Mary College Monthly, which combined the attributes of both magazine and newspaper. During his sophomore year, he was one of the two editors elected to the staff by the Philomathean literary society, his friend S. Otis Bland being the other. For the next two years, he edited the column called "Exchanges," a critical review of literary magazines from other colleges. At times, he doubtlessly found this uninspiring work, perhaps absolute drudgery; for the column, now and again, contains only a prefunctory notice or two. Nevertheless, touches of Cabellian wit are at times evident (e.g., Monthly, VI, 143-145). Since many of the individual contributions to the magazine are unsigned, it is nearly impossible to tell with precision how many of these are Cabell's. We do know, however, that Cabell signed some of his work with the pseudonyms "Clarence Ashley Bell" and "Charles Antrim Ballance."

This early work is important in tracing the inception of Cabell's ideas, and many of his later thoughts may be found in seminal form in the Monthly. In his prize-winning essay "The Comedies of William Congreve" (V, 40-44), written as a sophomore, he reveals the mature urbanity to suspend judgment coupled with a youthful disdain for thoughtless prudery:

> We are told [that the English Restoration] . . . is indecent; one must pass hastily over its actions, avoid mention of its people, and burn its writing--

> all this in forgetfulness of the fact that it is a
> logical outcome of the Commonwealth. For action
> produces re-action; the pendulum of Time momentarily
> caught back by Puritan cant and gloom, swings loose
> to the open gaiety and vice of the Restoration. . . .
> It is unwise to give hasty judgment. (p. 40)

Cabell seems to see in the Restoration a mirror of his own post-Victorian period, which was so vigorously trying to free itself from the Victorian concept of "respectability." He shows his keen sense of historical recurrence. But he goes on, tacitly drawing the parallel:

> Men have begun to observe and classify, they turn from
> creation to Criticism. . . . It is the Fashion to be a
> wit. . . . one must be able . . . to conceal indecency
> with elegant diction; manners are everything, morals
> nothing. (p. 41)

Under the guise of describing the Restoration wits, Cabell appears to be describing his own literary aspirations--though only in part. The final praise, in the essay, of Congreve's "all but perfect" style is perhaps an indication of one of the sources of his own.

In the same volume of the <u>Monthly</u>, over the pen name "Charles A. Ballance," Cabell published a poem called <u>The Blind Desire</u>. The second, third, and fourth quatrains read:

> Nay, 'tis not fitting that we should require
> Within this World but Raiment, Food and Fire;
> Powerless Atoms of Eternity
> Why should we hope to know of Something higher?
>
> This Knowledge could but add, not lessen, Woe;
> The Magian who To-day forms fire with snow
> Shares with the Sudra in Infinity.
> We come from Nothing and to Nothing go.

> So best consent, although with forced grace,
> Upon this dingy Ball to run our race
> Untrammeled with the thoughts of higher things,
> Until we reach the shadowy Stopping place. (p. 51)

The excerpt suggests that the young poet has been reading Edward Fitzgerald's <u>Rubaiyat</u>: the stanzaic form is the same, and the line "We come from Nothing and to Nothing go" seems to be a reminiscence of Fitzgerald's "the phantom Caravan [of life] has reach'd / The Nothing it set out from." On the evidence of this poem, we may list Fitzgerald as one of the sources of Cabell's cosmic skepticism.[4] As important as the source, however, is the attitude evinced. In his late teens, Cabell is beginning to feel the same tension between real and ideal apparent in his later novels. Man feels that it is "not fitting" (Jurgen would say "not just") that he should be trapped in a completely material world of "Raiment, Food and Fire," and yet, at the same time, he realizes the futility of seeking after "Knowledge" of "higher things." In this tension between real and ideal, man must somehow make the best of an infinitely poor situation.

By November, 1897, in an article on Dickens, "In Defence of an Obsolete Author" (<u>Monthly</u>, VII, 1-6), Cabell was already developing his theory of romance. "A novel, or indeed any work of art, is not intended to be a literal transcription from Nature. . . . Life is a series of false values. There it is always the little things that are greatest. Art attempts to remedy this. It may be defined as an expurgated edition of Nature" (pp. 3-4). In his later essay "On Telling the Truth" (VII, 53-55), he expands these ideas, concluding that "if we assiduously cultivate our powers of exaggeration, perhaps we, too, shall obtain the Paradise of Liars. And there Raphael shall paint for us scores and scores of his manifestly impossible pictures . . . and Shakespeare will lie to us of fabulous islands far past 'the still-vex'd Bermoothes,' and bring us fresh tales from the coast of Bohemia. For no one will speak the truth there, and we shall all be perfectly happy." And these ideas are finally brought to maturity in Cabell's book of essays, <u>Beyond</u> <u>Life</u>. Two more of his college essays, "Christopher Marlowe--Poet and Dramatist" (VI, 55-61) and "Black Spirits and White" (VII, 121-129), are also rewritten and included in this later volume.

In this limited space, having glanced briefly at a few of his prose works and one of his poems, we must leave his early work on the staff of the <u>William and Mary College Monthly</u> in order to examine the ugliness of reality.

Cabell's last months at the College were darkened by what has been called a "scandal," but was in actuality a series of vicious rumors. The origins and details of these rumors are, by their very nature, impossible to trace with any degree of accuracy. It has been conjectured that they grew out of a party given by Cabell "in honor of the Kappa Alpha fraternity" and followed by a dance on January 18, 1898.

The _Monthly_ described it as "one of the most delightful
social events of the season" (VII, 153-154). How did the
rumors begin? It has been suggested that everyone at this
gala event ended the evening too inebriated to recall what,
or if anything, had happened. But about the same time,
Charles Coleman fell from "a ladder, while arranging some
books in the up-stairs apartment of the library" (_Monthly_,
VII, 296-297), breaking his leg; he was seriously shaken.
His name was added to the rumors. Ellen Glasgow, who was
in Williamsburg in the spring of 1898 and who knew James
Cabell, suggests that the rumors had something to do with
homosexuality; but her source, as she says, was mere rumor:
"The leading middle-aged intellectual of the village, or
so I was told, had exercised a pernicious influence over
some of the students." Her account in _The Woman Within_
(pp. 130-133) is as distorted as the rumors themselves, for
she writes of the College's attempt "to root out and exter-
minate every trace of scandal . . . without proper investigation." The facts of the matter, taken from the Faculty
Minutes, tell a far different story.[5]

On March 31, more than two months after the supposed
"incident," the rumor first came to the attention of the
faculty. After the regular faculty meeting, they discussed
these rumors of "certain practices alleged to have been in
existence between students and between students and certain
college officers tending to the detriment of the College.

Waiting further information," they adjourned until the following day. The next day, Friday, April 1, the faculty with all due discretion resolved to investigate the matter "<u>as soon as</u> circumstances permit." However, before they could act on the resolution, on April 6, at 9:00 p.m., a faculty meeting "was called on request of certain students who desired an <u>immediate</u> investigation to be instituted, so that they might vindicate themselves from the charges of certain practices rumored to exist in College." The "certain students" were presumably Cabell and two other boys apparently mentioned in the rumors. The faculty "after some discussion" complied with the requested inquiry, and began to swear in students to give testimony at once. The next day, Thursday, April 7, the investigation resumed at 5:00 p.m. and lasted for the rest of the week.

The campus was in an incendiary condition, and, at one point on Friday, April 8, the students were near riot state in the Chapel, protesting that the faculty was persecuting fellow students while not considering its own dirty linen. Apparently, the rumor-victims were getting the support of their fellow students. Hearing of the student gathering, the faculty sent Professor Stubbs to quiet them. He assured them that the faculty was acting in all fairness; the students cooled down.

After a thorough investigation, and after carefully weighing the evidence over the weekend of April 12, on

Monday the faculty gave the opinion "that no evidence has been adduced before it sufficient to warrant a finding against" Cabell and his two friends. Whether other students were mentioned in the rumors, the Faculty Minutes do not say, but Cabell was cleared of all charges levelled against him by rumor.

After the exoneration of the students, however, the Minutes record that the name of Charles W. Coleman "frequently" had arisen in the investigation. Because of this fact, "the Faculty feels impelled to state that no evidence has been adduced before it sufficient to warrant a finding against him." Nevertheless, "On account of [his] recent accident," writes Coleman to the faculty about his fall in the library, "and the shattered condition of [his] system"--aggravated no doubt by vicious rumors--he had to resign his position as librarian. Unfortunately, this resignation has often been misconstrued as an admission of guilt by those who did not know of Coleman's accident and his extremely weakened condition: he could hardly walk.

Further, his letter of April 24, 1898, to his mother, may give us a clue to the origin of the rumors. In his letter, Coleman discusses his injuries both physical and spiritual, and immediately goes on to talk of religious matters. From his comments, Coleman was a religious liberal, believing that the essence of religion was in the "spirit" rather than in dogma or ritual; and somehow he seems to connect his present condition with his religious views. Is it possible that, though the rumors suggested "homosexuality," the actual incident (if there ever was an "incident") was a quarrel about religious liberalism? In the last days of Victoria, with the impact of Darwinism and Higher Criticism, religion was an explosive topic; and religious liberalism might easily be equated and confused in a small town with "other" abnormalities.

However, as the faculty reached its decision and cleared Cabell and the others of misconduct, the three boys appeared before the faculty and asked that their names be removed from the College rolls. Possibly moved by indignation that they should be subjected to suspicions of homosexuality, they said their stay in Williamsburg was no longer "pleasant or profitable." Their statement ends with an affirmation of their innocence.

Nevertheless, Cabell was not long away from the College, for his family felt that his resignation might be thought of as tantamount to an admission of guilt. Although Cabell's mother, Anne Branch Cabell, employed the services of William Preston, a lawyer, his help was virtually unneeded. Young Cabell wrote a letter to the Faculty, which was promptly passed on to the Board of Visitors, who immediately reinstated him as a student. Probably weary of the whole College, Cabell duly graduated with his B.A. on June 23, 1898.[6]

Although these final months may have been dark, much of Cabell's stay at William and Mary was "pleasant and profitable," and even the confusion and misery of this regrettable "incident" may have been of some value to the author who later so violently satirized the pretensions of society and depicted the terrors of mob-justice. But Cabell took more away from Williamsburg than a feeling of "savage indignation." He had been a scholastic success; his knowledge and learning were to prove invaluable to the writer of romance, and his creative work first published in the obscure <u>William and Mary College Monthly</u> is the seed from which the achievement of later years grew.

Notes

¹The materials for this study were drawn from various primary sources :William and Mary College Monthly (1894-98); the College Catalogue (1894-98); Faculty Minutes of the College of William and Mary (1894-98); the correspondence of Charles Coleman in the Earl Gregg Swem Library, College of William and Mary; "The Seven Wise Men of the College of William and Mary in Virginia," an address by James Southall Wilson; and private conversations with Margaret Freeman Cabell and Professor Edgar MacDonald.

²Joe Lee Davis, James Branch Cabell (New York, 1962), p. 151.

³Jurgen (New York, 1919), pp. 4-5.

⁴There were three copies of the Rubaiyat in Cabell's library. See Jean Maurice Duke, James Branch Cabell's Library: A Catalogue (Ann Arbor: University Microfilms, 1968), p. 121.

⁵Emmett Peter Jr., "Cabell: The Making of a Rebel," Carolina Quarterly, 14 (1962), 74-78, discusses this material, but comes to different conclusions. I wish to emphasize the element of conjecture involved in precisely locating the incident which led to the rumors of homosexuality. Cabell and Coleman attended both the party and the dance which followed it by some days.

⁶At William and Mary in 1898, the basic graduating degree was an L.I. (Licentiate of Instruction); the B.A. was a slightly advanced degree, entailing more academic work, though obtained in four years. It is also worth noting that, at the end of his junior year, Cabell received the Corcoran Scholarship for his academic achievement.

Chapter 2: The Growth of a Credo:
Beyond Life

After graduating from William and Mary, Cabell took a job as copyholder on the Richmond *Times*, and from 1899 to 1901 worked on the New York *Herald* and then on the Richmond *News*. These years were not uneventful for the young artist. During his first rather lonely months in New York, Cabell began writing to his cousin, Miss Norvell Harrison who lived close by in Brooklyn with her father. The correspondence grew into an epistolary love affair, some record of which is still extant at Duke University Library. Although it is impossible to say how far this relationship advanced, it was probably broken off in 1901. What effect the inconsequential affair had on young Cabell can only be guessed, but it is interesting to note that John Charteris, the chief speaker of *Beyond Life*, is given to using former love letters in his novels, while Norvell Harrison's brother, Henry Sydnor Harrison, author of the best-selling *Queed*, is uncompromisingly pilloried by Charteris as a literary hack.

On November 17, 1901, Cabell's cousin, John Scott, was brutally assaulted near the Cabell residence in Richmond and died some hours later. Cabell had, meanwhile, returned to Richmond, and local gossip suggested that he was implicated.

Rumor had it that Scott had been the lover of Anne Branch Cabell, James's mother, and that to protect his family's honor, the son had become an assassin. Although the police never effectively solved the murder, Scott was apparently beaten by the brothers of a girl from Buckingham, Virginia, whom he had seduced. Later, Cabell was able to put this incident to literary advantage in his novel The Rivet in Grandfather's Neck, but the rumors of his culpability seem to have upset him greatly and perhaps directly contributed to the ironic detachment which characterizes his style.

For the next ten years, Cabell worked as a subsidized genealogist, his investigations allowing him to travel in France, and Great Britain. His genealogical research is painstakingly and perhaps imaginatively recorded in Branchiana (1907) and Branch of Abingdon (1911). After concluding these volumes, Cabell joined the office staff of a coal mining company in West Virginia, where he worked until 1913. According to rumors, which in this case Cabell was happy enough to perpetuate, the private hours of these years were filled with delightfully libertine adventures. Nevertheless, on November 8, 1913, Cabell married Mrs. Emmett Shepherd, a rather well-to-do widow with five children, and settled down in "Dumbarton Grange" near Richmond to pursue his vocation as novelist.

By 1913, Cabell had published three novels and three collections of short stories. Out of these grew Cabell's major literary achievement, "The Biography of the Life of Manuel," which was collected into the eighteen-volume Storisende edition of The Works of James Branch Cabell (1927-1930).[1] When Cabell published his first novel, The Eagle's Shadow, in 1904, he had undoubtedly not planned the next twenty-six years of his artistic life. His conception of "The Biography" developed as he wrote, and his novels, short stories, poetry, and even reviews, were all worked into the grand design: a vast genealogical history of Western man from the Middle Ages to modern times. From the loins of Manuel the Redeemer of Poictesme (a mythic province in medieval France) comes the life-force which animates the main characters of "The Biography." Moving from France to England and finally to America, the life-force is still strong in Lichfield, Virginia (Cabell's fictive Richmond). Paralleling in many ways the actual genealogies he had compiled, "The Biography" is essentially comic, underscoring the discrepancy between man's ideals and the realities of his life. Cabell's ironic vision, however, is replete with somber overtones. Beyond Life is the first volume in the completed scheme, and here are introduced Cabell's main ideas. Its themes and its phrasing echo throughout "The Biography." The companion volume, Straws and Prayer-Books (1924), is the epilogue in which Cabell ties together the ideas of "The Biography," using the central concept of creative play. It is a much simpler book than Beyond Life, both in thought and in structure.

Some of Cabell's first critics, however, seem to have felt that the philosophic ideas upon which Beyond Life is built were, in the twentieth century, without interest or importance. Cabell's more intellectual contemporaries, on the other hand, seem to have found these ideas still very much alive. In the aftermath of the breakdown of traditional values in the nineteenth century, modern man was faced with a complicated ideological decision. A now-dominant science had undermined the religious assumptions of the former age, and those thinkers who refused to forego the idea that man was, at least in part, a creature of spirit were forced to accommodate the idea to a naturalistic universe. One might, of course, with the idealists, deny the existence of matter, but this solution could be congenial only to a few. Cabell's solution in Beyond Life is a compromise, a form of pragmatic idealism clearly resembling the thought of Jules de Gaultier in Le Bovarysme (1892, expanded 1902) and La Fiction universelle (1903), of Hans Vaihinger in The Philosophy of "As If" (1911, translated 1925), and of George Santayana in Interpretations of Poetry and Religion (1900) and Scepticism and Animal Faith (1923). Generally these thinkers accept a natural universe which is basically inimical to the desires of men, though, at the same time, they acknowledge man's need for something more than nature is able to provide.

Since the material world is not able to satisfy man's spiritual needs, man must himself construct "fictions," "noble delusions," "dreams," "mental structures." These are the ideals which man lives by in his determination not to accept a meaningless cosmos. As Cabell puts it, "we decline, very emphatically, to consider the universe as a whole,--'to encounter Pan,' as the old Greeks phrased it, who rumored that this thing sometimes befell a mortal, but asserted likewise that the man was afterward insane" (p. 93). The saving grace in this stubborn decision not to accept the primacy of matter is the possible miracle which may follow. By acting as if his dreams are true, man may cause them to become part of reality. "Indeed, the most prosaic of materialists proclaim that we are all descended from an insane fish, who somehow evolved the idea that it was his duty to live on land, and eventually succeeded in doing it. So, now that his earth-treading progeny manifest the same illogical aspiration toward heaven, their bankruptcy in common-sense may, even by material standards, have much the same incredible result" (<u>Beyond Life</u>, p. 115). In his lecture on "The Dilemma of Determinism," the pragmatic William James had similarly suggested that "possibilities may be in excess of actualities."

In Cabell's structure of ideas, the philosophical becomes closely linked with the literary. For Cabell, literary realism is another aspect of scientific materialism

--the cult of things--while his own version of pragmatic idealism is firmly linked with literary romance. According to literary historians, the debate into which Cabell entered in 1919 was begun about forty years before by William Dean Howells' essay, "Henry James, Jr." Although the initial controversy may be traced back to Defoe, and the main issues had been clear throughout the Victorian period, Howells' comments became the center of a debate over realism and romance which lasted well into the twentieth century. Cabell's distinction between the two is rooted in this literary debate. Most apparent are his similarities to Oscar Wilde's "The Decay of Lying" in <u>Intentions</u> (1891) and to Arthur Machen's <u>Hieroglyphics</u> (1902). Both Wilde and Cabell present the paradoxical idea that life imitates art, rather than art imitating life. It follows then that art should not record the facts of nature, and that the literary techniques of realism are misguided. Only the romanticist who creates his own fictional world is the valid artist. Machen and Cabell go on to insist that art is symbolic or emblematic. Machen writes: "it is not the business of the literary artist to describe facts--real or imaginary--in words: he is possessed with an idea which he symbolizes by incident, by a story of men and women and things" (Caerleon Edition, V, 77). Or, as Cabell interprets Machen, "all enduring art must be an allegory" (<u>Beyond</u> <u>Life</u>, p. 202).

In his discussion of the artist's point of view, Cabell is partially anticipated by W. H. Mallock's essay, "The Relation of Art to Truth," and in his off-beat view of "romance" by Frank Norris's essay, "A Plea for Romantic Fiction."

Cabell's relation to Robert Louis Stevenson's essays, "A Note on Realism," "A Gossip on Romance," and "A Humble Remonstrance," is more difficult to ascertain, and perhaps Stevenson is closer to Cabell in temperament than in thought. A comparison of Stevenson's bleak view of the universe in "Pulvis et Umbra" with Cabell's in <u>Beyond Life</u> suggests the similarity. For both, the cosmos is "an endless inconceivable jumble of rotary blazing gas and frozen spheres and detonating comets, where-through spins Earth like a frail midge. And to this blown molecule adhere what millions and millions and millions of parasites just such as I am, begetting and dreaming and slaying and abnegating and toiling and making mirth" (<u>Beyond Life</u>, p. 39). That two eminent modern romancers should share this world view certainly suggests something about the dark vision of modern romance.

The debate over realism and romance was still current when Cabell wrote <u>Beyond Life</u>. Literary magazines regularly published essays which explored their respective merits. In 1918, the year in which portions of <u>Beyond Life</u> were serialized in the Chicago Tribune, Wilson Follett, who was one of Cabell's admirers and correspondents, devoted the second chapter of his work entitled <u>The Modern Novel</u> to a discussion of romance and its relation to realism. He concluded that they were but different sides of the same coin. Edward Cox in his essay, "Realism Pure and Applied," which appeared in the <u>Sewanee Review</u> the following year, felt that there was a basic political distinction between realism and romance. Citing Wilde's "Decay of Lying" as adverse evidence, he suggested that realism is the ally of democracy and social reform, not just an artistic doctrine. His essay is of interest in that it highlights what otherwise might have escaped our attention--the political affiliation of Cabell's romance with skeptical conservatism. In Cabellian thought, man has yet to prove his political sanity or his ability to govern with any degree of efficiency. Cabell writes, "if you will attend a State Legislature, in particular, and look about you, and listen for a while, and reflect that those preposterous people are actually making and unmaking laws by which your physical life is ordered, you will get food for wonder and some perturbation" (p. 176). For Cabell at least, the literary creeds of realism and romance were linked not only with philosophical positions but also with political attitudes.

Before tracing the growth of <u>Beyond Life</u>, however, we should note one more element in Cabell's thought and its link with contemporary psychology and anthropology. The problem of the artist and the sacrifice of his life which he must make for his art is one of the central ideas in <u>Beyond Life</u> as it is also in Otto Rank's <u>Art and Artist</u>:

<u>Creative</u> <u>Urge</u> <u>and</u> <u>Personality</u> <u>Development</u> (trans. 1932). For the artist to dedicate himself to his art, he must forego the common life of ordinary mortals. The similarity between Cabell and Rank on this point may be entirely fortuitous; for "this cult of Art is very ancient, and began in days when goddesses were honored by human sacrifice" (<u>Beyond</u> <u>Life</u>, p. 95). Rank notes a similar idea in Schiller: "What would live in song immortally / Must in life first perish." Or, according to Cabell, "the elect artist" is "an economist" who resolves "to get enduring increment of his body, and by means of that movable carcass which for a while he partially controls, to make something that may, with favoring luck, be permanent" (pp. 89, 88). But the point here is that Cabell is exploiting not merely an ancient idea but one which the contemporary psychologist Otto Rank found to be of particular importance to the development of the artist. Throughout <u>Beyond</u> <u>Life</u>, Cabell is exploring, as a preface to his "Biography of the Life of Manuel," some of the most provocative questions of his time.

The growth of <u>Beyond</u> <u>Life</u> is complex. Various portions began as college essays at William and Mary, and were first published in the <u>William</u> <u>and</u> <u>Mary</u> <u>College</u> <u>Monthly</u> (1895-1898). They were thoroughly revised and incorporated into <u>Beyond</u> <u>Life</u>. "'Black Spirits and White'," became part of "The Witch-Woman," "Christopher Marlowe--Poet and Dramatist" part of "The Economist," "The Comedies of William

Congreve" part of "The Candle," "Richard Brinsley Sheridan" part of "The Mountebank," "In Defence of an Obsolete Author" part of "The Contemporary," and "Concerning the Old and the New" part of "The Arbiters." At times the revised portion bears little or no resemblance to the original essay, and part of the original essay on Congreve is used as an introduction to Wycherley in Beyond Life. Fortunately, the Congreve essay exists in at least three states, and a consideration of the successive changes may tell us something about Cabell's manner of revision. Cabell is describing the dramatic world Congreve has created:

[1] There is no longer any religion, any purity, and sacred ties; they do not belong in this country and must be left at the door. This is the land of Gallantry, of witty men and beautiful women, of elegance and epigrams; Virtue and Vice are both contraband. We have no laws--or rather we have only one law and that is "Live and Enjoy Life." Everybody is clever, everybody is happy; we are in a new Arcadia where Strephon wears powder and Phyllis is arrayed in the latest fashion of le Grand Monarque. Nymphs in patches and shepherds in peri-wigs roam happily through the drawing room of this Paradise, and warble their artless lays in the most perfect French. It is an ideal country; no civilization, no morals, no police--nothing but pleasure.

(William and Mary College Monthly,
V [1895-1896], 43)

[2] There is no longer any religion, any purity, any sacred tie of any sort; they do not belong in this country and must be left at the frontier. This is the Utopia of Gallantry; virtue and vice are both contraband. It is a beautiful country, and one that has been not infrequently maligned--or at least misrepresented. Detractors have complained that the sun never shines here; may be, but his place is filled--and well--by the light of many glittering priestlike candles. . . . Nor is an endless night an unendurable institution when one has a sufficiency of candles; their softer glow is even preferable

to the glaring sunlight when one is rouged--as all the
dwellers in this Utopia are. We are in a new Arcadia,
where Strephon wears powder and Phyllis is arrayed in
the latest mode from the court of Versailles; a new
Arcadia, between whose close-clipped hedges roam laugh-
ing nymphs in patches, pursued by magnificent shepherds
with red-heeled shoes and wonderful clouded canes. It
is an ideal country, where life, untrammelled by the
restrictions of morals or civilization or the police,
has no legitimate object save the pursuit of pleasure.

(<u>International</u>, X [1901], 297)

[3] True, there are, as always in travel, the customhouse
regulations to be observed: in this realm exist no
conscientious scruples, no probity, no religion, no
pompous notions about altruism, nor any sacred tie of
any sort, and such impedimenta will be confiscated at
the frontier. We are entering a territory wherein
ethics and ideals are equally contraband. For Congreve's readers make the grand tour of a new Arcadia,
where Strephon wears a peruke, and Phyllis is arrayed
in the latest mode from the Court of Versailles; and
where Priapos, for all that he remains god of the
garden,--about the formal alley-ways of which flee
bevies of coy nymphs (somewhat encumbered by brocaded
gowns) pursued by velvet-coated shepherds, who carry,
in place of vulgar crooks, the most exquisite of clouded
canes,--where the Lampsacene's statue, I repeat, has
been ameliorated into the likeness of a tailor's dummy.
It is a care-free land, where life, untrammeled by the
restrictions of moral codes, untoward weather, limited
incomes or apprehension of the police, has no legitimate
object save the pursuit of amorous pleasures.

(<u>Beyond Life</u>, pp. 136-137)

The three passages bear a recognizable resemblance to each other. At the same time, each revision adds a greater complexity to the picture, even though the candle passage of the second is excised in the third. The "nymphs in patches" become in the final revision "bevies of coy nymphs"; the varicolored canes of the shepherds are contrasted with "vulgar crooks," underscoring the reality to which Congreve's world stands opposed; and the travel motif is more clearly carried through the passage. Priapos, the god of both gardens and phallic potency, is introduced to preside over the "amorous pleasures," and the pursuit of the nymphs by the shepherds is significantly inserted between the two references to the god. Nevertheless, the sexuality is modified by Priapos's appearance in "the likeness of a tailor's dummy." The entire passage is a picture of an ideal in which reminders of the real are not wholly lacking. Throughout Beyond Life, the reader may catch reminiscences of the involuted prose style of Sir Thomas Browne or John Milton from whose Areopagitica the title comes: "a good book is the precious life-blood of a master-spirit, embalmed and treasured up on purpose to a life beyond life." Cabell himself felt that he was using "Greek sentences," that is, "holding the meaning of each sentence in solution for the last word to precipitate" (Between Friends, p. 10). The growth in stylistic complexity suggests a concomitant increase in the complexity of Cabell's thought and attitudes.

In the spring of 1917, when the United States entered the war against Germany, Cabell began work on Beyond Life; and the course of the writing may be followed through his letters. He wrote to his editor, Guy Holt: "I have quit fiction and am writing a book to elucidate my 'aesthetic creed'--being persuaded by you and Mr. [Wilson] Follett et al. that I have one--and have found that, subconsciously, it was just what I wanted to write."[2] According to the original plan, Cabell in his own person as novelist was to visit one of his creations, John Charteris, a minor character in Cabell's novels *The Rivet in Grandfather's Neck* and *The Cords of Vanity*. A novelist himself, Charteris was to speak to Cabell for ten hours, or through ten chapters. At Holt's suggestion this original plan was somewhat changed. Cabell writes: "The 'creator' business . . . , I will eliminate, and 'I' will be anonymous. The Prolegomena [Chapter I] . . . I will revise, with Townsend [a novelist in *The Cords of Vanity*] substituted for Charteris. . . . The references to my books will simply be removed. Only in one place do I foresee trouble, in the introduction of Mrs. Deland's letter, which is for my purpose quite requisite, but in this place I can equivocate along somehow" (*Between Friends*, p. 25). Although Charteris remains the speaker in *Beyond Life*, Cabell removed himself--except for some ambiguous hints--from the first edition. In the Storisende edition, however, he has partially returned (see p. 12). Margaret Deland's letter, probably the one quoted anonymously in "The Contemporary" (pp. 198-199), creates a bit of puzzlement if not obscurity. The Induction upon which she comments is Cabell's own "Auctorial Induction" to *The Certain Hour*.

The final chapter of *Beyond Life* gave Cabell most trouble; he called it "that interminable Tenth Chapter" (*Between Friends*, p. 39). The basic form of the chapter, however, was early decided upon. Cabell would put Holt's rebuttal of his ideas into the mouth of the interlocutor, and the rebuttal would be answered by Charteris. Since the interlocutor originally represented Cabell, he reveled in the irony of the situation; and, though this plan was modified, as we have just seen, the irony perhaps still remains. Although Cabell wrote to Holt that his rebuttal was "precisely what I wanted" (<u>Between Friends</u>, p. 20), Holt's words often suffer a sea-change. Perhaps one example will be indicative. Holt wrote to Cabell: "I had thought this was the province of youth, to view God and man with a doleful eye. But here am I upon the verge of twenty-six and with the wisdom of my generation within me, looking sadly down upon you from the rosy heights. You are all of a dozen years older than I and should of right be putting Pollyanna to the blush, by this" (<u>Between Friends</u>, p. 24). In Cabell's hands the passage becomes: "I had thought it the peculiar privilege of immaturity to view mankind and God with doleful eyes. But here am I, quick with the wisdom of my generation, compelled to shout denial to your doctrines from comparatively roseate heights, for all that you are by some twenty-two years my senior, and your opinions ought in consequence to be already gilded by a setting sun" (<u>Beyond Life</u>, pp. 252-253). But Holt's comments are not always so thoroughly rewritten, and some of the prose in the tenth chapter is his. The mixture of styles yields, possibly, a certain strangeness of texture to the last pages.

Although Cabell was constantly revising, an early draft of Beyond Life was sent to Holt late in 1917, and Burton Rascoe saw one version of the manuscript by March 7, 1918. Rascoe immediately arranged to publish it serially in the Chicago Sunday Tribune. On April 14, 1918, amid idealistic newspaper reports on the glories of the First World War, Rascoe began publishing edited selections from Beyond Life. Under various titles, the selections appeared each Sunday until August 11. Although textually similar to the first edition, the Tribune selections do reveal substantial variants from the later texts. We may only assume that these variants are not the product of Rascoe's assiduous editing. Nevertheless, we know that Rascoe was forced to cut Cabell's criticism of war--"the fact that we are sending our boys to death" (p. 180). Rascoe complained that freedom of the press was one of the emptiest of delusions in America, but there was nothing he could do. Beyond Life appeared in book form at the beginning of the next year, and Cabell sent Joseph Hergesheimer an advance copy on January 6, 1919.

Beyond Life is a series of ten essays, as Wilson Follett saw, of "calculated and preordained harmony, each essay coaxed into ten neat sections strung together and fitting like vertebrae, all the essays and all the sections falling into nicest adjustment to disclose a philosophy of life wrapped round a philosophy of letters. It is the book of a man whose supernal mathematic[s] ten times ten always make one, and one only." In the first editions, the sections of each essay are numbered from one to ten; but in the Storisende edition, Cabell numbered them consecutively, apparently to emphasize the unity of thought which Follett observed. The basic unit of structure is the individual section; and, throughout the book, the sections are arranged with consummate skill--distanced, balanced, ironically juxtaposed. The picture of wartime madness--"the nations flounder, and gabble catchwords, and drift, and strike out blindly"--in section sixty-nine is carefully placed with section seventy, an ironic and preposterous defense of patriotism. Section twenty-three introduces Marlowe as the creator of Faustus the sorcerer; and section thirty-one, echoing phrases from the earlier section, prepares for a fuller consideration of the dramatist and his work in sections thirty-three to thirty-five. These sections are alluded to in section eighty-three, which considers such "uneconomic" writers as Florence Barclay, Sydnor Harrison, and Harold Bell Wright. The progression is from sorcery, to artistry, to damning comparison. The division of the essays into sections tends to emphasize this kind of continuity, and the consideration of Cabell's artistic manipulation of the sections might be extended. The examples given, however, make the basic point.

Each essay has ten sections, and the structure of the individual essay is indicated by Cabell in a letter to

Holt: "I aimed in each chapter to have the literary 'appreciation' the octave of my sonnet, with some cosmic moral for my sestet. The Arbiter chapter, to divulge a secret, is two octaves run together when I had begun to tire of the book--Now it will have to be recast" (<u>Between Friends</u>, p. 25). Although Cabell felt that he "invented a new essay-form" (p. 9), the form is somewhat reminiscent of Carlyle's <u>On Heroes, Hero-Worship, and the Heroic in History</u> where the specific instance is used to draw a general conclusion about human affairs. Cabell's essays are, nevertheless, much more closely articulated into essay-sonnets, with rather strict divisions between the first six sections and the last four. The first part of each essay deals with specific examples, usually drawn from literary history, while the second moves on to generalizations connected in certain ways with the examples. In Cabell's hand, however, the form does not become stereotyped, and he is able to employ it quite unobtrusively. In the second essay, the first six sections trace the historical growth of the verbal arts from Greece to nineteenth-century England, while the last four sections deal with the growth of the Cinderella myth, the myth of man's ultimate triumph in the universe. The third essay begins with an historical and literary consideration of witchcraft and ends with a discussion of the "race-belief" in the supernatural lover, the witch-woman. Each of the essays is turned in this manner; thus, the fourth begins with Marlowe and Villon, and ends with "common-sense." The fifth deals with Wycherley and religion; the sixth with Congreve and literary immortality; the seventh with Sheridan and hypocrisy; and the eighth with Dickens, Thackeray, and human optimism. The ninth essay on "The Arbiters," however, seems never to have been fully brought into line with the others. Nine of its sections deal with critical evaluation and modern novelists, especially Booth Tarkington and Harold Bell Wright (from whose novel, The Winning of Barbara Worth, the epigraph of the essay is selected). Only the tenth and final section draws a general conclusion concerning man's dullness and vanity. Although this essay breaks the established pattern, it prepares for the misconception of the interlocutor in the epilogue, that Charteris is speaking only about the verbal arts.

Chapter one, the introduction, and chapter ten, the epilogue, do not fit as easily into this pattern as the other chapters, but they also proceed from the specific to the generalized application. The introduction begins with a description of Fairhaven (fictive Williamsburg, Virginia), the town in which Charteris lives, and goes on to describe Charteris's library. Since he is a fictional novelist himself, his library is well stocked with the works of other fictional novelists, as well as "the cream of the unwritten books," masterpieces by actual authors "planned and never carried through" (p. 10). Cabell explained to Rascoe that this collocation was "an attempt at honest confession as to my 'literary creditors'" (<u>Between</u> <u>Friends</u>, p. 35); and since some of the fictional authors are no longer familiar to the general reader, it may be well to list them and their creators: David Copperfield (Dickens), Lucien de Rubempré (Balzac), Mark Ambient (Henry James), Titus Scrope or Scroop (William De Morgan), Arthur Pendennis (Thackeray), Eustace Cleever, G. B. Torpenhow, and Richard Heldar (Kipling), Bartholomew Josselin (George Du Maurier), Gervase Poore and Lord Bendish (Maurice Hewlett), Colney Durance (George Meredith), Felix Wildmay or Mildmay (Henry Harland), Lucien Taylor (Arthur Machen), and Ernest Pontifex (Samuel Butler). The <u>Essay</u> <u>upon</u> <u>Castrametation</u> is by Jonathan Oldbuck in Scott's <u>The</u> <u>Antiquary</u>. The list is supplemented by the actual authors of "unwritten books": Stevenson, Keats, Milton, Coleridge, Spenser, Chaucer, Sheridan, and Marlowe. This rather long list of creditors provides a very interesting indication of Cabell's reading, and sets up a sounding board for the allusions to these authors which run throughout the book. Also, out of this fantastic library grows Charteris's general discussion of the "auctorial virtues of distinction and clarity, of beauty and symmetry, of tenderness and truth and urbanity" (p. 13). The chapter ends by introducing the concept of Romance with its attendant "dynamic illusions."

The epilogue is linked in form and in theme with the introduction. Out of the final discussion of the merits of Charteris's creed of literature and life proceeds a reaffirmation of the auctorial virtues set forth in the introduction. In the epilogue, however, these are seen as the qualities most worthy of possession in one's life, and the book ends with a statement of faith. "It may be that when our arboreal propositus descended from his palm-tree and began to walk upright about the earth, his progeny were forthwith committed to a journey in which to-day is only a way-station. . . . We are being made into something quite unpredictable, I imagine: and we are sustained, through the purging and the smelting, by an instinctive knowledge that we are being made into something better. For this we know, quite incommunicably, and yet as surely as we know that we will to have it thus." This desire to be "as we ought to be" is called Romance. "But when we note how visibly it sways all life we perceive that we are talking about God" (p. 270). In each of the essays, as well as the introduction and the epilogue, there is a movement from art to life. And we learn, finally, that those qualities which make the best artist and art are also those which make the best life.

In the structure of the whole book, these separate essays are as carefully balanced as the introduction and the epilogue. The second essay "Which Deals with the Demiurge" and the third essay "Which Hints at the Witch-Woman" both discuss ideas of man's transcendent value as a spiritual being. Though laced with Cabellian irony, these essays deal with concepts of man's individual importance in the cosmos--of his ultimate triumph and of his love for a divine mistress. We might call them discussions of archetypal myth. As if in reply, essay eight "Which Concerns the Contemporary" and essay nine "Which Defers to the Arbiters" place man squarely in the contemporary scene. Emphasizing realism rather than fantasy, these essays present the picture of man muddling through life, yet preserving the "dynamic illusion of optimism." His dullness and his vanity shield him from the direct knowledge of a hostile universe. In the first two essays, man was a child of divinity waiting for his divine lover; now he is merely a pitiable fool, whistling in interstellar darkness.

The four central essays may be seen as forming an intricate crisscross pattern. Essay four "Which Admires the Economist" and essay six "Which Values the Candle" are ironically related. In the first of these, Charteris discusses Marlowe and, subordinately, Villon, who are both willing to sacrifice themselves for their art. As Charteris says, the thrifty "artist is resolved to get enduring increment of his body" by producing the work of art which men will read forever (p. 88). The second part of the essay, however, is an ironic celebration of "common-sense" which allows man to do the work and enjoy the pleasures of the world. The final pages actually glorify the sacrifice of the artist. Commonsense may have its place, but in the overall view, the artist seems to espouse a nobler creed. Essay six begins with a discussion of Congreve, who found "the word-game, at which one plays for a dole of remembrance," not worth the candle (p. 145). The sacrifice of the artist is again considered, but this time it too is seen only as an illusion: "At such depressing moments of prevision, he [the artist] recognizes that this desire to write perfectly, and thus to win to 'literary' immortality, is but another dynamic illusion: and he concedes, precisely as Congreve long ago detected, that, viewed from any personal standpoint, the game is very far from being worth the candle" (p. 152). And so, Congreve did not wait for the witch-woman, but gave up his art, and devoted himself to seeking the pleasures of the flesh. The two essays, in the final analysis, stand as a destructive comment upon each other; neither approach to life, Marlowe's or Congreve's, seems quite worth the candle. Commonsense and sacrifice are equally illusions.

In their last sections, essay five "Which Considers the Reactionary" and essay seven "Which Indicates the Mountebank" discuss society and religion. The literary figure of "The Reactionary" is Wycherley, who, in reaction against the rule of Puritan which preceded the Restoration, developed the Comedy of Gallantry. Ironically, from the immoral reaction of the Restoration, Charteris turns to man's reaction against a purposeless, ever-restless nature. Man reacted, according to Charteris, by inventing the concepts of good and evil, and finally by creating the masterpiece of Romance, Christianity. Using these myths, man could in some way account for the random happenings of a chance universe. In essay seven, Charteris discusses the equally ambiguous growth of human government. The literary exemplar is Sheridan, the figure of the Mountebank, who pretends to be "as he ought to be" and thus is quite impeccable in his public functions. It is an easy step for Charteris to a general discussion of politics, for all government rests squarely on hypocrisy. To "save us from the driveling terror that would spring from conceding our destinies in any way to depend on other beings quite as mediocre and incompetent as ourselves," Romance "intervenes promptly, to build up a mythos about each of our prominent men,--about his wisdom and subtlety and bravery and eloquence, and including usually his Gargantuan exploits in lechery and drunkenness" (pp. 176-177). Thus men are saved from thoughts of an unfriendly universe and an incompetent society by the dynamic illusions of religion and great men.

These eight interrelated essays present anything but a sanguine picture of man's earthly existence. A creature of weakness, delusion, hypocrisy, man finds his life palatable only because of his blindness and vanity. Out of this conception of human nature, Charteris elaborates his economist's creed, that man is elevated not by his virtues but by his vices. The economy involved is that Romance, the demiurge, uses man's folly and mediocrity in a truly creative way. Man's very unreason leads to his elevation above the other animals, for man refuses to accept that he is simply an insignificant part of the material universe. Hypocritically acting in the expected manner, or playing the ape to the dreams given him by art, man slowly acquires those virtues which at first he only mimicked. It is this desire in man to become "as he ought to be" that Charteris calls Romance.

More than elaborating this concept of human economy, Beyond Life also introduces the three major attitudes toward life exemplified in the other volumes of "The Biography"; the Chivalric, the Gallant, and the poetic. "The cornerstone of Chivalry," says Charteris, "I take to be the idea of vicarship; for the chivalrous person is, in his own eyes at least, the child of God, and goes about this world as his Father's representative in an alien country" (p. 36). For the chivalrous person, life is a test, and it is his duty to perform as admirably as possible. The gallant person, on the other hand, sees life as a toy. "I have read," says Charteris, "that the secret of Gallantry is to accept the pleasures of life leisurely, and its inconveniences with a shrug; as well as that, among other requisites, the gallant person will always consider the world with a smile of toleration, and his own doings with a smile of honest amusement,

and Heaven with a smile which is not distrustful,--being
thoroughly persuaded that God is kindlier than the genteel
would regard as rational" (p. 101). Wycherley, Congreve, and
Sheridan are the three aspects of Gallantry, each giving up
his art for the pleasures of the world. Marlowe is the
exemplar of the poetic attitude, for the poet treats life
as raw material out of which he must make something more
durable than life. And, of course, this is the way of all
artists who are willing to sacrifice themselves for their art.
The ways of Chivalry, Gallantry, and poetry provide another
series of themes which help to unify the essays.

All the ideas of <u>Beyond Life</u>, however, are treated
by Cabell with a degree of ironic detachment. With Charteris
arguing his case, there is a great deal of difficulty in
determining the author's precise attitude toward his material.
His argument may be an ironic undercutting of the romantic
vision. Perhaps, he is saying, with Swift, that "this is
the sublime and refined point of felicity, called the possession of being well deceived; the serene peaceful state of
being a fool" in an alien universe. Or Cabell may see man,
even in the depths of his ignorance and vanity, as an admirable creature; for man stands defiant in a universe which
refuses to acknowledge his dream. Cabell's attitude appears
to be ambivalent, and even Charteris's ringing affirmation
of a force controlling man's destiny may be, in the light of
the preceding essays, either a piece of bitter irony or a

profound insight into the nature of things. As it stands, *Beyond Life* provides an excellent introduction to Cabell's thought in "The Biography of the Life of Manuel." "The Biography" also deals with the ambiguities and the paradoxes of human life. It is a chronicle of chivalry, gallantry, and poetry; of vanity, dullness, and hypocrisy; of aspiration and compromise; of admiration, pity, and scorn. It is a history of human life in all its greatness and in all its tragic futility.

Notes

[1] All references to Cabell's works are to this edition, unless otherwise noted.

[2] *Between Friends: Letters of James Branch Cabell and Others*, ed. Padraic Colum and Margaret Freeman Cabell (New York: Harcourt, Brace, 1962), p. 9.

Chapter 3: Cabell's Sources: The Mirror
of Illusion and Reality

Cabell's library has been catalogued by Maurice Duke, and the catalogue confirms what we had already presumed, that the author read widely and well. Indeed, much scholarly effort has been spent in the attempt to discover Cabell's sources, to trace the learned author in his reading. But perhaps the image that has most vexed source-hunters is Cabell's mirrors. In Cabell, the mirror is often associated with pigeons, and the last chapter of Warren A. McNeill's Cabellian Harmonics is devoted to a discussion of mirrors and pigeons.[1] James Blish in a brief note suggested that Cabell's mirror is the "Mirror of Solomon," a magic device manufactured with the aid of the blood of white pigeons.[2] Both McNeill's and Blish's discussions are inconclusive, but Blish does realize that the mirror is most important; the pigeons are incidental.

Before discussing Cabell's use of the image, we should emphasize that the mirror is a recurring symbol throughout literature. Lewis Carroll comes immediately to mind. Alice finds that her looking glass is "just a bright silvery mist" and that she can enter through the mirror into "Looking-glass House," into another reality. In his Book of Imaginary Beings,

Jorge Borges recounts the Chinese myth "that goes back to the legendary times of the Yellow Emperor. In those days the world of mirrors and the world of men were not, as they are now, cut off from each other. . . . Both kingdoms, the specular and the human, lived in harmony; you could come and go through mirrors."[3] Abraham Merritt in his short story, "Through the Dragon Glass" (1917), unites the strains of Carroll and Chinese myth. His hero, Herndon, finds that the Dragon Mirror has the ability to grow "misty" until it is "nothing but a green haze" and that he can enter into an oriental world of love and horror--a world from which he does not return.[4] Working in another vein, Lawrence Durrell uses mirrors throughout the <u>Alexandria Quartet</u> to suggest the various planes of reality which reflect, refract, distort our vision of the "real" world. In a way, Durrell's mirrors symbolize his art. In his poem "Ars Poetica" in <u>Dreamtigers</u>, Borges writes: "At times in the afternoons a face, / Looks at us from the depths of a mirror; / Art must be like that mirror / That reveals to us this face of ours."[5] Both Durrell and Borges employ the old idea that art is a mirror of reality. In his <u>Dictionary of Symbols</u>, J. E. Cirlot discusses the diversity of the mirrors' "meaningful associations," and two of these associations are relevant in the present context. The mirror is "a symbol of the imagination" and hand-mirrors are specifically "emblems of truth."[6] The mirror has a dual symbolic nature, suggesting both imagination and reality.

This brief survey of the divers artistic uses of mirrors should warn us against seeking a unique source for Cabell's looking glasses and from demanding a single interpretation of the mirror's meaning in Cabell's work. With a wealth of mirror lore before him, Cabell was able to select various aspects of this lore and to create a complex symbol. When Cabell was subsequently asked to explain the secret or the meaning of his mirrors, he had no single answer. He could only evade the question, and then in his next book complain of unsophisticated readers who seemed to miss the meaning of his work.

This warning notwithstanding, I would like to speculate about a possible source for one Cabell mirror. J. W. Thomas has pointed out that Jurgen's Florimel comes from Spenser's _Faerie Queene_, Book III (probably the false Florimel who is much more likely to be a vampire),[4] and it may be further suggested that Cabell's Garden between Dawn and Sunrise finds an analogue in Spenser's Temple of Venus (Book IV), where (Mark Rose writes) "multitudes of true lovers and friends take their decorous pleasures among the even ranks of trees." It seems plausible to assume, then, that when Cabell was writing _Jurgen_, he had Spenser's poem on his mind. In _Jurgen_, Merlin possesses "a small mirror, about three inches square," and Jurgen looks "into the little mirror" (p. 125).[8] It seems apparent from the conversation that follows, that Merlin's mirror allows him to see the truth about

Jurgen. Spenser describes the power of Merlin's glass in the Faerie Queene:

> The great Magitian Merlin had deuiz'd
> By his deepe science, and hell-dreaded might,
> A looking glasse. . . .
>
> It vertue had, to shew in perfect sight
> What euer thing was in the world contaynd,
> Betwixt the lowest earth and heauens hight,
> So that it to the looker appertaynd. . . .
>
> (Faerie Queene, III.ii.18-19)

Thus, Jurgen is confronted, by means of this mirror, with the truth about himself and his dealings. The suggestion that Merlin had such a mirror may be traced to Spenser, and ironically the mirror appears in that portion of the Faerie Queene which celebrates the virtue of Chastity.

But Jurgen's father Coth in The Silver Stallion meets with a similar looking glass in the hands of Yaotl. Coth is presented with the truth about Manuel when Yaotl sits "thinking and looking into the scrying stone," i.e., "a mirror surrounded by green and yellow and blue feathers" (pp. 105, 87). Yaotl's "thought" takes "form very slowly as a gray smoke" and out of the gray smoke appears Manuel to explain the nature of things to Coth (p. 105). Admittedly the scene is quite different from the confrontation of Merlin and Jurgen, but both father and son are forced to face a certain reality which they would rather evade. The present scene with Yaotl also indicates that the mirror is connected with the imagination and with creativity. When Yaotl ends his "thinking" and puts "aside the scrying-stone," Manuel disappears (p. 111). The mirror is indispensable to the recreation of Manuel.

The Mirror of Caer Omn (Romance) seems to be more akin to Carroll's and Merritt's; the mirror becomes "a warmish golden mist" (p. 77). Through this Mirror in the land of Dersam (Dreams), Gerald goes on a journey into the world of romance. Finally, when he is being trapped by Evarvan of the Mirror, he breaks the spell, the artistic spell of romance, by the "runes of common-sense." He recites a list of hard and cold facts, and the illusions of Romance melt "back into the moonshine of the Sacred Mirror of Caer Omn" (p. 97). The mirror does not force Gerald to face reality as would the mirrors of Merlin and Yaotl.

Obviously, the mirror of Queen Freydis, the Mirror of the Hidden Children in Something About Eve, is not the same as the Mirror of Caer Omn. The mirror of Queen Freydis must "be faced by those persons who venture into the goal of all the gods and men" (p. 11), i.e., Antan, yesteryear, which bears the suggestion of oblivion. Glaum warns Gerald, "I would not meddle with that mirror. Even in the land of Dersam, where a mirror is sacred, we do not desire any dealing with the Mirror of the Hidden Children and with those strange reflections which are unclouded by either good or evil" (p. 11, emphasis mine). Again we have returned to the mirror of reality which does not have the moral qualities known only to men, but which simply records in its fleeting way the ravages of time, our passage into Antan and oblivion. The Mirror of Caer Omn is its direct opposite.

But in other places, the mirror seems to be the symbol for an obscure, but shared knowledge. In *The Cream of the Jest*, both the "personage" and the "prelate" show Felix Kennaston their small hand-mirrors in much the same way that Merlin shows his mirror to *Jurgen*. They seem to expect a response, but unfortunately for Kennaston, he seems unable to grasp the meaning of the mirrors.[9] His bewilderment is also ours, and perhaps we should accept this effect as the one desired by Cabell. Reality is puzzling; Romance-- Kennaston is a writer of romance--tries to order and give meaning to Reality.

Cabell compounds our puzzlement about mirrors by adding the element of pigeons, often three pigeons. Of course, in Mexico where pigeons were undoubtedly not available, Yaotl decorates his mirror with colored feathers. In certain cases, the mirror seems to work only in the presence of pigeons, as when Jurgen prepares to regain his lost youth and when Gerald prepares to return home to Lichfield. Jurgen rejects the blue bird, which, as Conway Zirkle has pointed out, is the symbol of happiness, and accepts the pigeons.[10] But what do the pigeons symbolize? In *The Cream of the Jest*, Kennaston calls them the "birds of Venus" (p. 79), equating pigeons with doves. By extension, the pigeons take on the

symbolism of Venus herself: beauty and love. In order to
make the mirror function, these qualities must be present.
In <u>Jurgen</u>, this symbolism seems possible, for Jurgen rejects,
to begin, happiness in order to recapture the beauty and
love of his youth (i.e., Dorothy). Sereda's mirror is in
one way like the Mirror of Caer Omn, for it allows Jurgen
to step through it into the romantic past. But in others,
the mirror is a mirror of Lytreia in which the hero comes to
see himself and to investigate the ideals he has held and
their worth. It is like Morvyth's mirror in <u>The Silver
Stallion</u>, a "gleaming and over-wise counselor" (p. 37).

My suggestion is, then, that the mirrors in Cabell
are complex symbols and that each must be examined in the
immediate context of the narrative and not simply as part
of a general motif. This suggestion is valid, I think, for
any recurring element in Cabell's work. Further, I believe
there are two kinds of mirror: the mirror of art (Caer Omn)
and the mirror of reality (Queen Freydis's mirror). In one,
we step through the mirror into Lewis Carroll's world of
dreams and romance; in the other, we see ourselves as a
reflection of reality in our passage toward Antan and death.
The mirrors reflect the duality of Cabell's Janus-faced
world where man is continually caught between the reality
and the dream.

Notes

[1] Warren A. McNeill, *Cabellian Harmonics* (New York: Random House, 1928), pp. 92-103.

[2] James Blish, "The Mirror and Pigeons Resolved," *Kalki*, 2 (1968), 97.

[3] Jorge Luis Borges, *The Book of Imaginary Beings* (New York: Dutton, 1969), p. 105.

[4] A. Merritt, "Through the Dragon Glass," in *The Young Magicians*, ed. Lin Carter (New York: Ballantine, 1969), pp. 126-143.

[5] Jorge Luis Borges, *Dreamtigers* (Austin: University of Texas Press, 1964), p. 89.

[6] J. E. Cirlot, *A Dictionary of Symbols* (New York: Philosophical Library, 1962), pp. 201-202.

[7] J. W. Thomas, "More Holes Filled," *Kalki*, 4 (1970), 132.

[8] All references to Cabell's works are to the Storisende Edition (New York: McBride, 1927-30).

[9] See the next chapter for a fuller discussion of mirrors in *The Cream of the Jest*.

[10] Conway Zirkle, "The Blue Bird," *Kalki*, 4 (1970), 120.

Chapter 4: Cabell's <u>Cream of the Jest</u>
and Recent American Fiction

When, in 1940, Joe Lee Davis set about to predict the course of American fiction in the following decade, he chose Cabell's phrase "resolute frivolity" as descriptive of the 20's, a period which Davis was using as a key to the future.[1] "In one sense," resolute frivolity "meant the affectation of a deliberate skeptical irony as a mask for underlying uneasiness and disillusion. . . . But, in another . . . , the 'resolute frivolity' of the 20's was a genuine manifestation of the play spirit" (p. 39). As John Barth's character Joe Morgan asks: "where the hell else but in America could you have a cheerful nihilism, for God's sake?"[2] The difference between Cabell's resolute frivolity and Barth's cheerful nihilism is, of course, an index to a shift in tone in American fiction and generally in American culture.

This shift in tone was predicted by Davis. He felt that America was prepared "for a new kind of 'resolute frivolity.'" As a medium for this new frivolity, he looked for

> a revival of the fantasy novel which characterized the 1920's. I think this type of novel will be needed . . . for the writers and readers who are profoundly disturbed

> by the meaning of it all and doubtful, beneath any
> seeming of assurance, of the value of life itself.
> The "resolute frivolity" of some possible fantasist
> of the 40's, some American Franz Kafka . . . , may
> mask a bitterness far more intense than Cabell's and
> may soar to heights of mysticism that Cabell was
> incapable of achieving. (p. 44)

The accuracy of Davis's prediction is remarkable. Of course, his dating was off by a decade or so; possibly delayed by World War II, the new frivolity did not emerge until the 50's and 60's with the advent of Ellison, Gaddis, Heller, Barth, Vonnegut, Pynchon, Percy, and those writers who mix despair with bitterness and comedy with fantasy. Although these authors are as different as they are similar, taken as a group they apparently mark a new direction in American fiction.

But as Davis's commentary suggests, the direction is <u>not that new</u>, and the blend of skepticism, fantasy, and comedy which we feel is unique in recent fiction is also distinctly Cabellian. From one point of view, at least, Cabell is technically and thematically the forebear of the fiction of the 50's and 60's, and not the mauve humorist he is often said to be.

A good deal of this assertion can be illustrated by considering a central novel in Cabell's works, <u>The Cream of the Jest</u> (1917).[3] The novel purports to be the spiritual biography of Felix Bulmer Kennaston, a novelist, written by his acquaintance, Richard Fentnor Harrowby, a manufacturer of soaps and cosmetics. Harrowby sets himself the task of understanding and explaining how Kennaston changed from a minor poet to a major novelist, and in the course of his inquiry into the sources of verbal genius, he becomes (influenced by Kennaston's preoccupations) interested in the relationship of the artist to his creation.

After a brief foreword, Harrowby narrates Kennaston's rejected conclusion to his best-selling novel, The Men Who Loved Alisoun. Ironically, this rejected ending becomes the beginning of Harrowby's exploration of Kennaston's psyche. The rejected ending is set in medieval France, in Cabell's mythical Poictesme, and deals with the marriage of La Beale Ettarre and Sir Guiron des Rocques. However, more important than the marriage is Horvendile's plot to introduce Maugis d'Aigremont, Guiron's enemy, and his men into the castle at Storisende. During the blood bath which follows, Horvendile contrives a series of startling reversals and finally confronts Maugis, the character he has ultimately betrayed. "As knave and madman, Ettarre saw the double-dealer and his dupe confront each other. . . . In the hand of Horvendile a dagger glittered; and his face was pensive, as he said: 'My poor Maugis, it is not yet time I make my dealings plain to you. It suffices that you have served my turn, Maugis, and that of you I have no need any longer. You must die now, Maugis'" (pp. 24-25). In the next pages, we learn that we have not witnessed a murder, but a piece of allegory. Horvendile tries in vain to explain to Ettarre and Guiron that

he is a surrogate for Kennaston--"I am that writer of romance"
--that Horvendile is a demiurgic character. "And you, messire
--and you also, madame--and dead Maugis here, and all the
others who seemed so real to me, are but the puppets I fashioned
and shifted, for a tale's sake, in that romance which now
draws to a close" (p. 27). But Ettarre and Guiron cannot
believe they are merely the creatures of a monstrous "plot."
They can only consider Horvendile a madman and exile him from
Poictesme. And so Horvendile-Kennaston regretfully leaves
his fictive world and the fantasy ends.

    This opening fantasy is a perfect overture for the
fictional biography which follows. Beyond introducing important themes of the novel--marriage, the inaccessibility of
true beauty, double-dealing--it prepares us for the ironies
of creation which are central to Cabell's thought. In this
introductory tale, "a world's creator was able to wring only
contempt and pity from his puppets--since he had not endowed
them with any faculties wherewith to comprehend their creator's nature and intent" (p. 42). The artist, it appears,
stands in god-like relationship to his creatures.

    But Kennaston's god-like superiority is only apparent.
As his imaginative life becomes more vital, he realizes that
his creation had more meaning than he, at the time, had
thought. "What was it Maugis d'Aigremont had said?--'I have
been guilty of many wickednesses, I have held much filthy
traffic such as my soul loathed; and yet, I swear to you,

I seem to myself to be still the boy who once was I.'
Kennaston understood now, for the first time with deep
reality, what his puppet had meant; and how a man's deeds
in the flesh may travesty the man himself" (p. 87). By
accident, as it were, the artist can create characters who
speak more wisely and have greater insight than the artist
himself. If the creatures of the introductory tale cannot
understand Horvendile, apparently Horvendile-Kennaston did
not always understand the characters he was creating.

Later, when Kennaston is living his dream life with
Ettarre[4] (in much the same way that Kurt Vonnegut's Billy
Pilgrim lives with Montana Wildhack on Tralfamadore), he
initially believes that she is his own creation, an emanation from his novel. However, as he achieves a deeper understanding of the creative process, he comes to believe "that
perhaps the Ettarre he loved was not the heroine of his
book inexplicably vivified; but, rather, that in the book
he had, just as inexplicably, drawn a blurred portrait of
the Ettarre he loved, that ageless lovable and loving woman
of whom all poets had been granted fitful broken glimpses"
(p. 105). For Kennaston she becomes the quintessential
loving woman, and his literary creation was merely an attempt
to capture that super-reality and place it in his own fictional world. Since the author is both world-creator and
finite being, he cannot, paradoxically, be expected to

understand the fullness of his own creation. Further experience is necessary for the artist to gain the requisite understanding.

Quite naturally, Kennaston's (and by extension Harrowby's) inquiries into the relationship of creator to creature lead to religious speculations. If the artist's business is to create ordered existence, then the symmetry inherent in life-forms is a sign that an artistic creator is at work in the universe. God is simply "Kennaston's fellow craftsman," the earth, "that corner of the studio wherein the God was working just now, and all life . . . a romance the God was inditing." But how does the Judeo-Christian religion square with the idea of life as an artistic romance?

> That the plot of this romance began with Eden and reached its climax at Calvary, Kennaston was persuaded, solely and ardently, because of the surpassing beauty of the Christ-legend. . . . He could imagine no theme more adequate to sustain a great romance than this of an Author suffering willingly for His puppets' welfare; and mingling with His puppets in the similitude of one of them; and able to wring only contempt and pity from His puppets. (p. 159)

The situation, as Kennaston recognizes, is parallel to his own as artist. From this perspective, in this strangely ironic world of art, Horvendile is analogous to Christ in God's creation. But Horvendile (an anagram for "horned evil") is a strangely diabolic Christ, and surely there is something sinister in the Cabellian analogue.

However, if the series of artists includes divinity, it does not end there. Harrowby's relation to Kennaston is also the relationship of artist to creation. Like Kennaston's feelings for the upright Guiron, Harrowby's for Kennaston are ambivalent. In a rather long digression (which of course is not digressive), Harrowby brings himself to admit, "I never quite liked Felix Kennaston" (p. 44). To Harrowby, he was "inadequate" (p. 43). Ironically, the artist who has set himself the task of explaining Kennaston has no sympathy for the character he is explaining. Furthermore, like Kennaston the artist, Harrowby does not fully understand the story he is telling. In his discussion of Kennaston's "Sigil of Scoteia," Harrowby insists, "the design upon these covers, as I have since been at pains to make sure, is in no known alphabet." But the reader, from his point of vantage, need only turn the Sigil upside down to see that the "curlicues and dots and circles" are really English (p. 238). Obviously Harrowby, because of his ignorance, is not a completely reliable narrator. Again, like Horvendile-Kennaston, he withholds knowledge from his creation. Although Harrowby knows (or thinks he knows) that the Sigil is in reality the top of a cold cream jar, he does not tell Kennaston. He allows him to retain his belief that the jar top is a magic sigil. In Harrowby we meet the ambivalence, the ignorance, and the duplicity which seem to characterize the Cabellian artist-as-demiurge. Entering the story as he does, Harrowby is analogous to both Horvendile and Christ.

In the novel's structure, the demiurges are kept distinct from the artist-gods, and, this being so, we must necessarily postulate that Cabell is the artist-god for whom Harrowby is the demiurgic character. The series then goes from reality (Cabell), to virtual reality (Harrowby, Kennaston), to fiction (Horvendile), to divinity (God), and each step takes us further from verification. There is here, as in a good deal of recent fiction, a progressive movement into the realms of fantasy, a delicate and inseparable blend of the fictive and the real, of what appears to be fact and what seems to be illusion.[5]

But Cabell not only enters the novel as the demiurgic Harrowby, he also enters as Kennaston. Kennaston's country home, Alcluid (Alcluith), is synonymous with Dumbarton, Cabell's home.[6] It would seem that Cabell wished to be identified, in part, with Kennaston. The point is that Cabell enters his novel not only as artist (Harrowby) but also as subject (Kennaston), and thus the complex relationship between creator and created is internalized. And internalization of experience becomes one of the novel's dominant ideas: "your true right tragedy is enacted on the stage of a man's soul" (p. 229). Kennaston and Harrowby are both parts of Cabell.

For Kennaston, man lives in a completely subjective, isolated world. "Perhaps--he mused--perhaps in reality all heads were like isolated planets, with impassable space

between each and its nearest neighbor. . . . a perpetual
isolation, for all the fretful and vain strivings of humanity
against such loneliness, was probably a perdurable law"
(p. 113). But man is not only isolated from his fellow man,
he is also isolated in time. "How poignantly strange it
was that life could afford him nothing save consciousness
of the moment immediately at hand! Memory and anticipation,
whatever else they might do--and they had important uses, of
course, in rousing emotion--yet did not deal directly with
reality". Kennaston recurrently contemplates the tenuous-
ness of his contact with the outside world. All he has is
his own "evanescent emotions and sensations" (p. 119).

Moreover, the reality which man does experience is
generally dull and uninspired. Although Kennaston's relationship with his wife is dreary, he finds that the dullness
of homelife is compounded in high places. The conversation
during his visit to the "personage"--modelled on Cabell's
visit to Teddy Roosevelt at the White House--is a tissue of
commonplaces and banalities. In the novel, the discussion of
the weather becomes symbolic of man's inability to achieve a
certain distinction in his life (pp. 73, 208). Man's isolation from this dull reality can hardly be of any great
consequence.

The buffer of isolation notwithstanding, man does
need assurance that there is something more than bare reality,
the gray dullness of universal similarity. The answer, for

Kennaston, is the mystical Sigil of Scoteia, which in the world of reality is the top of a cold cream jar. Created for Harrowby's cosmetic company by the semi-literate Mr. Flaherty, the top is in Harrowby's opinion "meaningless" (p. 238). In contrast, the Sigil teaches Kennaston that "everything in life is miraculous" (p. 240). For him, the Sigil is extremely meaningful. The opposition between Harrowby the realist and Kennaston the fantasist is important, for the novel in large part deals with the interplay of reality and fantasy, and these two principles--reality and imagination--are symbolized by the Mirror and the Sigil.

Much ink has been employed in the attempt to explicate Cabell's use of Mirrors and Pigeons since Warren McNeill underlined the problem in Cabellian Harmonics.[7] Most of the approaches have been hampered by their insistence that the mirror is a constant symbol throughout Cabell's work and that the best way to understand the symbol is through a study of Cabell's sources. Both of these assumptions seem wrong to me. Instead, the mirror is a multiple symbol, and the best way to understand the meaning of the mirror is to examine the contexts in which it appears. In The Cream of the Jest, I submit for openers, the mirror is a symbol of reality.

Both the "personage" and the "prelate" show Kennaston small mirrors which they carry, and both of them ask him if he raises pigeons. He tells the prelate:

> I could find it in my heart to believe it the cream of an ironic jest that you great ones of the earth have tested me with a password, mistakenly supposing that I, also, was initiate. I am tempted to imagine some secret understanding, some hidden coöperancy, by which you strengthen or, possibly, have attained your power.
> (p. 101)

The prelate deftly evades a direct reply, instead noting that Kennaston has no taste for public life. The passage is certainly enigmatic, and Cabell practices his customary reluctance--an almost ritual reluctance[8]--to explain.

Later, however, when Kennaston is time-traveling with Ettarre, he notices that Oliver Cromwell also carries a "small square mirror." Ettarre observes that men of power do not love "the sigil and the power the sigil gives." Rather, "that mirror aids them. In that mirror they can see only themselves. So the mirror aids toward the ends they chose, <u>with open eyes</u>" (p. 190, italics mine). Kennaston-Horvendile is told that he can never "penetrate these mysteries now. . . . The secret of the mirror was offered you once, and you would not bargain" (p. 190). Precisely when the secret of the mirror was offered remains a mystery to the reader, but the meaning of the mirror is now fairly apparent. The mirror allows the realist to see himself as he actually is, and thus the mirror symbolizes external reality, the surface of things.

The association of the mirror with pigeons is more puzzling, but I think Cabell points to the answer when he has Kennaston call pigeons "the birds of Venus" (p. 80). The birds belong to the goddess of love, and by extension, the pigeon itself symbolizes love. In the context of the mirror, I suggest that the pigeons indicate self-love. The men of power who gaze so intently, so fondly into the mirror of reality are experiencing the grand passion. They are looking at their own images.

In contrast to the great ones of the earth, Kennaston "looked into a steel mirror, framed with intertwined ivory serpents that had emeralds for eyes, and found there a puzzled stranger" (p. 108). As Harrowby-Cabell points out, it is the "sardonic point of his story . . . that the person you or I find in the mirror is condemned eternally to misrepresent us in the eyes of our fellows" (p. 44-45). For Kennaston, the mirror does not furnish a clear vision of reality, but simply a false distortion.

If the mirror represents the reality principle, then the sigil is its opposite, being the door to fantasy, imagination, the extra-real. The sigil is associated with the goddess Isis, and in contrast to the masculine mirror, it is connected predominantly with females. Instead of seeing himself as he _is_ in the sigil, Kennaston imagines himself as he would like to be. The aging, childless writer changes into the dapper young man of action, Horvendile, who is always in his twenties, and always at the centers of Western civilization. It is significant that, as Kennaston loses the power of the sigil, he sees himself in his wife's mirror:

"the mirror showed him a squat insignificant burgess in shirtsleeves, with grizzled untidied hair, and mild accommodating pale eyes, and an inadequate nose, with huge nostrils, and a spacious naked-looking upper-lip" (p. 220). Obviously this mirror image contrasts brutally with the youthful spirit of Kennaston the artist. When his wife denies any knowledge of the sigil and throws it away, their eyes meet "in the mirror" (p. 224). It is finally in the presence of the mirror that the sigil loses its power, and Kennaston is cut off from the source of his genius.

The source of that genius--and it is the novel's self-proclaimed purpose to elucidate the burgeoning of genius in Kennaston--is Ettarre, the lady of the Sigil. She is, as Kennaston tells her mockingly, "a daughter of subconsciousness or of memory or of jumpy nerves or, perhaps, of an improperly digested entrée" (p. 52). Possibly she is all of these, though Kennaston's digestive and nervous systems will not concern us here. Ettarre is, of course, closely related to the high-born maiden of nineteenth-century literature, the unattainable, isolated woman, like Tennyson's Lady of Shalott, who is both external muse and internal psyche. Ettarre is, in one of her aspects, the personification of Kennaston's creative urge, "a daughter of subconsciousness."

But she is also the daughter of memory. Kennaston comes to believe that Ettarre was constructed in his imagination from his wife's "youth and purity and tenderness and serenity and loving-kindness" (p. 222). Of course, this is Kennaston's loving meditation upon his wife, and he conveniently forgets that Muriel Allardyce, who in some ways is Kennaston's alter ego, had once appeared to him as Ettarre: "Her eyes were the eyes of Ettarre. All the beauty of the world seemed gathered in this woman's face" (p. 181). Apparently Muriel also contributed to the making of his Muse. But even further, Ettarre is the Platonic Idea of woman; she is the feminine principle, the perfect woman whom the male always pursues and never attains. The memory involved here goes deeper than the memories of individual women the artist has known.

Still and at the same time, there is something "sinister" about Ettarre, as Horvendile himself points out at the beginning of the novel.[9] The touching of Ettarre is for Horvendile always a kind of "suicide," and when she comes to him for the last time, she comes as Death. Kennaston's time-travelling with Ettarre is all into the Past. Unlike Billy Pilgrim's adventures in time, there are no projections into the future, no promises of future distinction. And yet, Ettarre and her Sigil have apparently rescued Kennaston from the dullness of everyday reality, from isolation and loneliness, from the limitations of time.

Nevertheless, this rescue involves Kennaston's further isolation from his wife. Although he may be saved from the pressures of reality, he loses the attendant pleasures, the real pleasures of a real world. In a way, the world of illusion that he has built to protect him from the dullness of reality keeps him from recognizing his wife's innate beauty. Within a year of this recognition, Kathleen dies. The true cream of the jest, then, may not be that the Sigil of Scoteia is really the top of a cold cream jar, but that the Sigil which gave Kennaston the imaginative life he desired was concurrently depriving him of the fullness of life "in the flesh."

Cabell ironically undercuts what appears to be a central idea of his novel, that imagination can adequately protect us from an inimical reality. After carefully constructing an orderly artistic universe where artist-god and his demiurge mediate between reality and imagination, Cabell calls all order and all meaning into question. Kennaston's orderly and meaningful universe, the one he is driven to accept by his needs and desires, is based on the premise that creation is the product of a rational creator. But in the chapter "By-Products of Rational Endeavor," Cabell implicitly suggests that man's accomplishments, from the discovery of gunpowder to the founding of Protestantism in England, are not at all based on reason; for the creator in each case had no idea of what he had really created. Here there is a stress on the irrational element in creation, a stress which casts skeptical doubt on a rationally created order in the universe.

Kennaston shares in this irrationality. Although he may, on one level, be considered a creative artist, on another, as Harrowby is constantly aware, he may be the victim of hallucination brought on by self-hypnosis. His schizophrenic tendencies, the split between Kennaston and Horvendile, force us to believe that his creativity stems from an abnormal psyche. He stands in a long line of twentieth-century literary protagonists who are mentally abnormal.

As I have hinted recurringly in this essay, Kennaston looks forward to Vonnegut's Billy Pilgrim, who also finds reality too much for him and who must create, through literature, another dimension in which to exist.[10] For both Kennaston and Pilgrim, time-travel is the answer. Kennaston, influenced by his uncle's esoteric library, travels into the past; Pilgrim, influenced by Kilgore Trout's science fiction, travels to Tralfamadore, a planet inhabited by creatures built like plumbers' friends. (Pilgrim also travels into the past, but his most significant travels are into a science. fiction-like future.) In their travels, Kennaston and Pilgrim meet the women of their dreams, Ettarre and Montana Wildhack. In both cases, time-travel gives the characters a way of coping with an unbearable reality and at the same time keeps them from dealing in an adequate way with the real world. They enter the ambivalent land of the lotus eaters. The parallels between Cabell and Vonnegut are arresting, and force us to consider further Cabell's relationship to recent fiction.

Kennaston's search for patterns of meaning, a way of sustaining himself in an aimless universe, clearly adumbrates the searches in Thomas Pynchon's V,[11] and The Crying of Lot 49. In his first novel, Pynchon's character, Stencil, attempts to give his life structure by forcing all the V's he finds into a meaningful configuration. Pynchon here seems to be mocking the search for order in a random universe. Oedipa Maas, the heroine of The Crying of Lot 49, represents the other side of the coin. In order to break out of her initial isolation, Oedipa seeks a pattern in reality, a pattern which may or may not be there, and the search leads her to the edge of paranoia. Her paranoia is related thematically to the schizophrenia of Kennaston. The cosmic allegory of Kennaston's quest for pattern also looks forward to Barth's Giles Goat-Boy and The Sot-Weed Factor. Kennaston as much as Giles or Eben Cook is adrift in a perplexing and aimless reality. The quest for meaning at the edge of madness, the theme of a good deal of contemporary fiction, is a major Cabellian preoccupation.

Further, Cabell foreshadows the use in recent fiction of the insidious plot, the idea of a strangely contrived conspiracy in which humanity is caught. With his series of artist-gods and demiurges, Cabell suggests that perhaps not only the characters in fictional Poictesme are controlled by a demiurgic Horvendile; for if indeed the universe is part of an ordered creation, we too are merely part of a divine or diabolic masterplot. Cabell is followed by such diverse works as <u>The Sirens of Titan</u>,[12] with its cosmic conspiracy to provide Salo with a part for his spaceship; <u>The Sot-Weed Factor</u>, in which Henry Burlingame contrives a bewildering and perhaps meaningless series of conspiracies; <u>The Crying of Lot 49</u>, where a conspiracy against the federal mails suggests a psychic drama as well as a national crisis; and <u>Love in the Ruins</u>,[13] with its cosmic conspiracy using Thomas More's lapsometer. Cabell, as well as Vonnegut, Barth, Pynchon, and Percy, realizes that the quest for meaning may lead us to a meaning that we do not wish to face. We are caught in a paradoxical situation: for our lives to have meaning, we must run the risk of being controlled from outside, or being trapped in a "plot"; for our lives to be free, we must endure the possibility of a meaningless, random universe. It is this central and desperate paradox that Cabell shares so vitally with the authors of the 50's and 60's.

In Cabell, then, we find a good deal that looks forward to the fiction of the last two decades. This is not to say, of course, that there are no differences. Cabell's emphasis on a graceful urbanity led to a mannered style which could not be further from the simplicity of Vonnegut or even the facile colloquialism of Pynchon. And perhaps the

differences in style point to a more fundamental difference.
The loss of hope is certainly an idea recurring in Cabell,
but his world was far less hopeless, say, than the world of
Vonnegut. Death is a constant theme in Cabell, but the horror
of Vonnegut's mass destructions is absent. Cabell hated war
perhaps as much as Vonnegut, but he did not directly experience the bombing of Dresden. He was not a survivor of an
insane violence. Obviously the tone of American fiction has
changed along with the temper of the nation. But my point
is not that Cabell is completely at one with the more recent
writers of fiction, but that he must be seen as their distinguished forerunner in theme and technique--and thus as
a pivotal figure in twentieth-century American literature.

Notes

¹Joe Lee Davis, "The American Novel: The Prospect for the 1940's," Michigan Alumnus Quarterly Review, 47 (1940), 38-44.

²John Barth, The End of the Road (1967; rpt. New York: Bantam, 1969), p. 47.

³The text used in the present study is the 1927 London edition published by John Lane. See James Branch Cabell: A Bibliography, by Frances Joan Brewer (1957; rpt. Freeport, New York: Books for Libraries Press, 1971), pp. 36-37.

⁴The name "Ettarre" (which Cabell saw as an anagram for retreat and perhaps treater) comes directly from Tennyson's "Pelleas and Ettarre," Idylls of the King. Cabell's Ettarre is not the lascivious woman depicted by Tennyson.

⁵John Barth is especially noteworthy here. In Giles Goat-Boy (Garden City, New York: Doubleday, 1966), Barth moves intricately from fictive reality (Publisher's Disclaimer, Cover-Letter to the Editors and Publisher) to the reality of fiction (the four Reels of the story) back to fictive reality (the final tapes and footnote). For the same kind of fictive-real blending, see Barth's Chimera (New York: Random House, 1972), pp. 191-193, 248, et passim. Barth, like Cabell, also likes to introduce himself as a demiurgic character into the story. See, e.g., Chimera, pp. 8-9, and Giles Goat-Boy, p. 314. The passage in Giles suggests further that Henry Burlingame in The Sot-Weed Factor, revised ed. (Garden City, New York: Doubleday, 1967), and the doctor in The End of the Road are Barth's demiurges. For this whole group of ideas and techniques, one might compare Norman Mailer's film Maidstone which is part fiction, part reality and in which Mailer, the director, plays the role of a film-director, Norman Kingsley.

⁶See William D. Jenkins' note, "Alcluid Unclouded," Kalki 3 (1969), 52.

⁷Warren A. McNeill, Cabellian Harmonics (New York: Random House, 1928), pp. 92-103. See also James Blish, "The Mirror and Pigeons Resolved," Kalki: Studies in James Branch Cabell, 2 (1968), 97, who believes that Cabell is referring to the Mirror of Solomon, and Emmett Peter, Jr., "Another Mirror for Pigeons," Kalki, 3 (1969), 88-91, who points to Burton's translation of The Book of the Thousand Nights and a Night.

⁸The phrase "ritual reluctance" is found in Thomas Pynchon's The Crying of Lot 49 (Philadelphia: Lippincott,

Notes

1966), p. 71. Applied there to The Courier's Tragedy (a play-within-the-novel), the phrase fits Pynchon's and Cabell's style equally well.

⁹The Cream of the Jest, p. 12: "that perfect beauty which is . . . somehow touched with something sinister."

¹⁰Kurt Vonnegut, Jr., Slaughterhouse-Five (New York: Delacorte, 1969), also uses the convention of the fictional biography.

¹¹Thomas Pynchon, V. A Novel (Philadelphia: Lippincott, 1963).

¹²Kurt Vonnegut, Jr., The Sirens of Titan: An Original Novel (1959; rpt. New York: Dell, 1971).

¹³Walker Percy, Love in the Ruins: The Adventures of a Bad Catholic at a Time Near the End of the World (New York: Farrar, 1971).

Chapter 5: Cabell and Barth:

Our Comic Athletes

In _Some of Us: An Essay in Epitaphs_ (1930), James Branch Cabell turned a critical eye on the American literary scene of the previous decade, a scene in which he, as author of the multi-volumed "Biography of the Life of Manuel," was a chief actor. Writing specifically of those who had come to artistic maturity in the twenties, he observed:

> It was their melancholy privilege to see with the eyes of maturity the world's civilization collapse like a popped paper bag. Their juniors yet had time to forget; their elders were well past learning anything. They only had seen with the eyes of maturity poor human nature left naked in every quarter of earth and gibbering in a fashion to embarrass any ape that had heard of Darwin. None of these writers, I suspect, has ever quite recovered from the spectacle; before its terrors some turned away to pessimism and the others to a resolute frivolity, but each one of them saw that there is no cure for being human and not any recipe for human living. That perception was perhaps unavoidable. What has followed, though, is that no one of these writers has peddled any recipe such as archbishops might smile on and pedagogues applaud.

The passage perfectly suggests the emotional climate of the twenties, and Cabell's reaction to it. On the surface, such a climate may seem hardly conducive to humor, but Cabell points out that one of the alternatives for a novelist in the twenties was what he calls "resolute frivolity," the way of the humorist. And Cabell greeted his crumbling world with exactly this formula. But the resolute frivolity which Cabell vaunts is not simply an alternative to "pessimism," for it is a frivolity which takes pessimism as its base, playing arpeggios upon despair.

Resolute frivolity, then, is a way of dealing with pessimism. Although art can provide no answers, it can teach us how to smile, and even how to laugh, and ultimately how to endure.

Twenty-eight years after the publication of Cabell's essay, John Barth in <u>The End of the Road</u> (1958) has his characters, Joe Morgan and Jake Horner, face a similar cultural crisis. For them, no moral imperatives exist; the world of objective values has collapsed. "When you say good-by to objective values," Joe explains, "you really have to flex your muscles and keep your eyes open, because you're on your own. It takes <u>energy</u>. . . . Energy's what makes the difference between American pragmatism and French existentialism--where the hell else but in America could you have a cheerful nihilism, for God's sake?" Barth's "cheerful nihilism" is a darkening and deepening of Cabell's "resolute frivolity." But Barth's implied reaction to cultural disintegration is similar to Cabell's. When one's civilization collapses like a popped bag, one greets the devastation not with tears, but with a paradoxical jest--"a cheerful nihilism, for God's sake."

Moreover, Cabell's "resolute frivolity" and Barth's "cheerful nihilism" point to a similarity in artistic approach as well as a similarity in attitude. One might call Cabell and Barth the comic athletes of American fiction. They are the players of literary games. In his essay, "The Literature of Exhaustion," Barth contends that once all the possibilities of an art form have been exhausted, then either a new form must be created, or the artist must ironically turn the exhausted possibilities back upon themselves. The ironic alternative--and this is Barth's own method--is essentially a game, a form of play within old rules. In this verbal playing Cabell is Barth's forebear. "I can play with words rather nicely," says a typical Cabellian hero.

If Barth's <u>Sot-Weed Factor</u> ironically proves that the eighteenth-century novel ignored its funeral in 1800, then Cabell's early stories prove that the pseudo-medieval romance was also alive and well at the beginning of our century. But Cabell's handling of this form is even more ironic than Barth's handling of the eighteenth-century novel. Cabell's first illustrator, Howard Pyle, the distinguished defender of Robin Hood's authenticity, firmly believed that the Middle Ages was "the age of faith." Yet he continually found in the pages of Cabell's romances allusions to the lack of both strict morality and faith. Pyle finally decided that he could not in conscience illustrate any more of Cabell's stories. The anecdote tells us something about both Pyle and Cabell. In Cabell's hands, pseudo-medievalism became a vehicle for an ironic attack on pseudo-respectability, and his use of the form became an elaborate game.

Further, Cabell and Barth like to play the game of infinite regression in and out of the fictive and the real, putting their fictions within fictional frameworks which pretend to be "reality." Smilingly they ask, "Where does the fiction begin and the reality end?" In <u>Lost in the Funhouse</u>, Barth's anonymous character remarks that "assaults upon the boundary between life and art, reality and dream, were undeniably a staple of his own and his century's literature as they'd been of Shakespeare's and Cervantes's, yet it was a fact that in the corpus of fiction as far as he knew no fictional character had become convinced as had he that he was a character in a work of fiction." But Cabell is again first in the field. In <u>The Cream of the Jest</u>, the fictional author, Felix Kennaston, does indeed come to believe that he is a character in a work of fiction, that life itself is a form of Romance, and that God is the master artist. In fact, in this novel, Cabell uses a series of authors: Cabell (or his persona, the "real" author); Harrowby (the putative "real" author who is writing a biography of Kennaston); Kennaston (a fictional best-selling author whose fiction forms part of his own biography); and God (the divine author, who may be either fictional or real, as the reader wishes). Each of these authors apparently feels the need to embody himself within his fiction as a kind of demiurgic character. God embodies himself as Christ in his fiction; Cabell uses Harrowby as a demiurge; Harrowby enters his biography in propria persona; and Kennaston assumes the name and bodily form of Horvendile. Barth also is fond of playing with the same kind of regression, as, for example, in <u>Giles Goat-Boy</u>, with its pseudo-editorial apparatus--Publisher's Disclaimer, Cover-Letter to the Editors and Publisher, and Footnote to the Postscript to the Post-tape --which lends a fictional frame to the central fiction. And, as much as Cabell, Barth likes to place himself as demiurge in the middle of the novel's action. The description of Harold Bray with his "round, black-mustachioed countenance" distinctly resembles the picture of Barth himself on the dust jacket of <u>Giles Goat-Boy</u>, and Bray's former occupations, psychotherapist and "minor poet," remind us of the doctor in <u>The End of the Road</u> and Henry Burlingame (the initials are the same) in <u>The Sot-Weed Factor</u>. In a final similarity, both authors like to suggest the diabolic nature of their demiurgic characters. Cabell's favorite demiurge, Horvendile, is anagrammatic for "horned evil," and Burlingame has "the eyes of Eden's serpent." Cabell and Barth seem to be suggesting that creation is not exactly a function of the greatest good, that creation--rather ironically--is made and directed by a diabolic power.

However, I am not trying to imply that the games which Cabell and Barth play are mere exercises in irony. As paradoxical as this assertion may seem, they are playing basically serious games. Johan Huizinga has taught us that the playing of games may be fun--"a free activity"--but play may also be deadly serious. Play promotes, according to Huizinga, "the formation of social groupings." It is a matrix for culture. If this is so, may not the playing of Cabell and Barth be a perhaps unconscious effort to reconstruct the civilization which they see collapsing about them? Possibly. But I would suggest that the games of Cabell and Barth are a conscious way of getting at an intellectual solution to the problems of man in a transitory world. Although Christian theology has always emphasized man's impermanence, the twentieth century has added to that idea the concept of relativity. Formerly we might acknowledge man's physical impermanence while yet believing in his absolute spiritual value. Now we are given to feel that no values are absolute.

Cabell's most well-known novel, <u>Jurgen</u>, is basically an exploration of values. After Jurgen has tried a variety of approaches to human value, he is left "inch deep in fine white ashes." In the end, all his pretensions to distinction --esthetic, sexual, and religious--have come to this. But a vision of man's universal unimportance has been vouchsafed to Jurgen earlier in the novel by the brown man with queer feet. The brown man is Pan, whose name Cabell interprets as "all." The confrontation of the egotistical Jurgen with Pan is comic, but the essential meaning of the passage is not: "You would have me believe that men, that all men who have ever lived or shall ever live hereafter, that even I," says Jurgen, "am of no importance!" For Jurgen it is a hard fact to accept, and indeed he does not accept it. "I will not," he tells the brown man, "believe in the insignificance of Jurgen. . . . I seem to detect in myself something which is permanent and rather fine." Face to face with meaninglessness, he asserts his personal worth.

In a similar passage in Barth's <u>Sot-Weed Factor</u>, Henry Burlingame and Eben Cooke share a vision of "Blind Nature" howling outside, a vision of universal madness. And Burlingame's solution resembles Jurgen's: "One must needs make and seize his soul, and then cleave fast to't," he tells Eben, "or go babbling in the corner; one must choose his gods and devils on the run, quill his own name upon the universe, and declare, ''Tis <u>I</u>, and the world stands such-a-way!' One must <u>assert</u>, <u>assert</u>, <u>assert</u>, or go screaming mad. What other course remains?" To avoid madness, both Burlingame and Jurgen agree, one must postulate one's importance, even if such a postulate flies in the face of the facts. Perhaps both owe something to Vaihinger's "als ob" philosophy. However, for Cabell and Barth the "as if" solution is at bottom a comic one, presented with irony, for in the contexts of the novels man is in no way important. The problem remains, and will not be solved by a mindless, comic affirmation of human worth.

Since both authors mock man's assertions of his importance in the universe, they are at pains to mock his myths and his history--those elements of our culture which are always handled so humorlessly by the professional theologians and historians. Cabell's *First Gentleman of America* is a fictive history of Don Luis de Velasco, born Nemattanon, a prince of the Ajacan Indians. A shadowy figure in the history books, Nemattanon--if this is indeed his Indian name-- was found by a Spanish exploratory force in Northern Virginia; he returned with them for Christian baptism in Mexico City, where he gained the name of Luis de Velasco, traveled to Spain where he met King Philip, came back to the New World, lived in Florida for several years, and finally went home to his own tribe with a group of Spanish priests. After massacring the priests, he led his people inland to avoid Spanish reprisals. This fascinating historical incident has been ignored, Cabell theorizes in *Let Me Lie*, "because it did not involve persons of Teutonic ancestry." It is, of course, a basic American myth that "Anglo-Saxons" were responsible for the exploration and colonization of North America; and it is generally forgotten, Cabell notes, that St. Augustine is older than Jamestown.

Cabell takes the bare bones of Nemattanon's history and turns it into, as his subtitle indicates, "a comedy of conquest." In the novel, there is some doubt about the parentage of Nemattanon: his father is reputedly the god Quetzal, who has set himself up as the chief deity of the Ajacans. But Quetzal is probably--though Cabell never tells us--a disguised Spanish soldier, one Vasco de Lerma, who was forced to flee Mexico after rescuing Cortés from the Indians. The story is recounted by the present Viceroy of Mexico:

> Lerna pulled Cortés out of the mud, still upside down, like a cork coming out of a bottle. The rude fellow re-inverted, and he propped upright, like a sack of coals, the great Marquis of the Valley. . . . after he had looked at the mud-covered Marquis, who happened at this instant to have a disturbed crayfish hanging on to his left ear, this Lerna laughed.

As Pedro Menéndez comments, "To laugh was not pardonable." But laughter is indeed the only reasonable way to respond to the antics of Spanish conquest. Later in the narrative, Menéndez, whose son has been sacrificed to a local deity by the Indians of Caloosa, marches against them. But instead of punishing the Caloosans for their sacrificial practices, Menéndez marries the Caloosan princess, Antonia, a part-time prostitute and full-time nymphomaniac, thus committing bigamy, in order, so he seriously claims, to bring the Indians to Christianity. And thus Cabell forces us to take another look at the Spanish conquest of America and to see it for what it was, a comedy of pride and stupidity.

Cabell's Luis de Velasco is the imaginative ancestor of Barth's character, Henry Burlingame III. Like Don Luis, Burlingame is an Indian prince of European ancestry, who has gained all the sophistication Europe has to offer. Further like Don Luis, he returns to his tribe and disappears from history. It is interesting to note that Barth's three Burlingames are almost the only nonhistorical characters in The Sot-Weed Factor, and even more interesting to speculate whether or not Barth was directly using the history of Don Luis for his story of Henry Burlingame III. However that may be, Barth handles American history with the same humor that characterizes Cabell's recreation. The wonderful colony to which Eben Cooke aspires to be poet laureate turns out to be "poor shitten Maryland," and Eben's proposed epic of colonization turns into a satire. Furthermore, Barth contrasts the accepted history--John Smith's True Relation, a book which Cabell humorously questions in Let Me Lie--with the Secret Historie supposedly written by Smith, but actually a Barthian reconstruction.

In his Secret Historie, Smith offers a partial description of Maryland as he found it: "It doth in sooth transcend the power of my pen, or of my fancie, to relate the aspect of this place, so forsaken & desolate & ill-appearing withal; a sink-hole it is, all marshie and gone to swamp. . . . It is forsooth Earths uglie fundament, a place not fitt for any English man." Smith himself is a satyr, and the Indians he meets are as sexually depraved as he. Hicktopeake's queen--shades of Cabell's Antonia--welcomes his advances, but demands "first some payment, saying, That she was not wont to bestowe her charms for naught." The noble savage queen, however, does not win in her bargaining with the randy Smith. Like Cabell, Barth turns conquest into comedy. The proud history of a proud people becomes a burlesque, and we must darkly smile at what it <u>must</u> really have been like. America was not founded by a race of demigods, but by a species of adventurers, sinners like ourselves. As Cabell notes, a "native Virginian historian . . . discovered intrepidly, without needing any mere evidence to abet him, that, 'no doubt,' every one of the jailbirds transported into the Colony of Virginia, during the period of establishment, had been convicted unjustly." The myth of foundation lives on, but Cabell and Barth smile sardonically at the delusions of national grandeur.

The two authors also use more universal myths in their fiction--the myths of the hero and his apotheosis into godhead. Barth indeed has become known for his ironic recreations of classical epic myth, the "Menelaiad," the "Perseid," and the "Bellerophoniad." The emphasis on "phoni" in the final title perhaps indicates Barth's dominant attitude. Cabell had earlier dealt quite explicitly with the myth of the hero in <u>The Silver Stallion: A Comedy of</u>

Redemption (1926). The series of stories which makes up
this volume is concerned with Dom Manuel's fictive
apotheosis into a Christ-figure and the reaction of his
"disciples," the Fellowship of the Silver Stallion. Cabell
leaves us in no doubt about Dom Manuel and his men: "for
there was never . . . a hardier gang of bullies than was
this Fellowship of the Silver Stallion in the season that
they kept earth noisy with the clashing of their swords and
darkened heaven with the smoke of the towns they were
sacking." Yet out of this reality grows the myth of
Manuel's sainthood as Redeemer of Poictesme and his expected Second Coming. Nor does Cabell underestimate the
power of this myth. Manuel's spirit is fetched back to
earth to explain the meaning of it all to the sturdy
realist, Coth of the Rocks, Jurgen's father:

> For Poictesme has now, as every land must have, its
> faith and its legend, to lead men more nobly and more
> valorously than ever any living man may do. I, who
> was strong, had not the strength to beget this legend:
> . . . it has been created by the folly of a woman
> [Manuel's wife] and the wild babble of a frightened
> child [Jurgen]; and it will endure.

Mundus vult decipi: the world desires to be deceived.
Although strong men like Coth will never delight in the
fantasies of myth, these fantasies do have their function
as exemplary tales leading men to more noble actions.

Barth deals at length with the myth of heroism in
Giles Goat-Boy. Initially Giles is convinced that he is
a "grand tutor," a prophet-hero, and the novel traces the

multiple vicissitudes of his education and his progress toward enlightenment, for him a relative point of view. He finally comes to believe that all distinctions are fruitless. However, his wife, Anastasia, has developed a "great nagging faith" that Giles is a legitimate Grand Tutor, and she has invented "Gilesianism"--a new religion--which, she feels, "will cure the student body's ills." Their putative son (Giles has his doubts about the father) will, according to Anastasia, "establish 'the New Curriculum' on every campus in the University." As in The Silver Stallion, the object of adulation realizes that his status as religious hero is a by-product of his wife's imaginative faith.

In his short story, "Night-Sea Journey," Barth returns to the concept of the hero and puts his ironic monologue in the mouth (so to speak) of a sperm navigating the dark passage toward the egg. In the beginning we learn that the sperm has "imagined night-sea journeying to be a positively heroic enterprise." But one of his fellow sperm develops a skeptical attitude toward the business of heroic endeavor and suggests that "the genuine heroes . . . were the suicides, and the hero of heroes would be the swimmer who, in the very presence of the Other [i.e., the egg], refused Her proffered 'immortality' and thus put an end to at least one cycle of catastrophes." The speaker seems to accept this cynical stance, but, perhaps driven by his own life-force, ends the story chanting, "Love! Love! Love!"--as he prepares to unite with the egg and lose his identity as a sperm. The chant has been read by some as a positive affirmation of the power of love, but surely in the skeptical context, such an affirmation--like that of Jurgen or Burlingame--is ambiguous. Love is merely another delusion to live by and the sperm's final affirmation is comic.

In sum, Cabell and Barth both seem to suggest that the intellectual "recipe for human living" is a comic acceptance of reality followed by a stoical resignation. At the conclusion of Jurgen, the eponymous hero returns to his home and his ill-natured wife. At the end of The Sot-Weed Factor, Eben and his sister retire to the family plantation and comparative solitude. Although the innocent may cling to myths and ambitions, the experienced must take an urbanely negative point of view in which nothing matters very much.

Nevertheless, there is an emotional difference between Cabell's "resolute frivolity" and Barth's "cheerful nihilism." Though Cabell may laugh at our need for myth, he sees the possibility that myths may be culturally valuable. Barth treats myth with a similar irony, but seems to see no possibility of a positive effect in the acceptance of illusions. In The End of the Road, Jake Horner finds mythotherapy, which involves the acceptance of a mythic role, to be worse than useless; it leads only to death. The loss of hope is certainly a recurring idea in Cabell's artistic universe, but his world is far less hopeless than the world of John Barth, where, ultimately, nothing is of value.

Selected Bibliography

James Branch Cabell wrote more than fifty books. Most of his fiction written before 1930 was collected into the eighteen-volume Storisende edition, The Works of James Branch Cabell (New York, 1927-1930). This edition contains his best-known novels: The Cream of the Jest: A Comedy of Evasions (first published 1917), Jurgen: A Comedy of Justice (1919), Figures of Earth: A Comedy of Appearances (1921), The High Place: A Comedy of Disenchantment (1923), The Silver Stallion: A Comedy of Redemption (1926), Something About Eve: A Comedy of Fig-Leaves (1927), along with volumes of short stories, The Line of Love: Dizain des Mariages (1905), Gallantry: Dizain des Fêtes Galantes (1907), Chivalry: Dizain des Reines (1909), The Certain Hour: Dizain des Poètes (1916), and poetry, From the Hidden Way: Dizain des Échos (1916). Originally published in book form in 1919, Beyond Life: Dizain des Démiurges is the first volume of the edition. In Modern Library format, it had achieved a second edition in 1923 with a perceptive Introduction by Guy Holt. Another book of interrelated essays, Straws and Prayer-Books (1924), complements Beyond Life and acts as an epilogue to "The Biography." The final volume of the edition, Townsend of Lichfield: Dizain des Adieux, is a kind of catch-all containing essays, short novels, sonnets, and Cabell's bibliographical account, "Evolution of the Biography." In this account, Cabell notes that several essays written at William and Mary were revised and included in Beyond Life. They are: "'Black Spirits and White,'" William and Mary College Monthly, VII (1897-1898), 121-129; "Christopher Marlowe--Poet and Dramatist," VI (1896-1897), 55-61; "The Comedies of William Congreve," V (1895-1896), 40-44; "Richard Brinsley Sheridan," VI (1896-1897), 235-239, "In Defence of an Obsolete Author," VII (1897-1898), 1-6; and "Concerning the Old and the New," VI (1896-1897), 285-289. In his description of these essays, Cabell seems to divide the last into two parts: "The Old and the New, and Concerning Criticism." "Concerning the Old and the New" deals with criticism, and no essay named "Concerning Criticism" appears in the William and Mary College Monthly. Cabell's essays in the Monthly were published either anonymously or over a pseudonym such as "Charles Antrim Ballance." The Congreve essay was later rewritten for The International: An Illustrated Monthly Magazine of Travel and Literature, X (1901), 291-298.

Perhaps the best individual critical comments on Beyond Life are Wilson Follett's "Ten Times Ten Make One," Dial, LXVI (1919), 225-228; Guy Holt's Introduction to the Modern Library edition (mentioned above); and Joseph Warren Beach's "The Holy Bottle," Virginia Quarterly Review, II

(1926), 175-186, reprinted in his The Outlook for American Prose (Chicago, 1926), pp. 63-80. Follett deals with both the structure and the ideas; Holt gives a brief, but interesting commentary; and Beach provides a searching analysis of Cabell's style and its affinities. Floyd Dell, "The Importance of Being an Artist," Liberator, II, iii (March, 1919), 48-49, compares Cabell's ideas to those of H. G. Wells, and finds Beyond Life unimportant and uninteresting.

Cabell's later fiction is grouped into three trilogies: "The Nightmare Has Triplets," "Heirs and Assigns," and "It Happened in Florida." Smirt: An Urbane Nightmare (New York, 1934), Smith: A Sylvan Interlude (New York, 1935), and Smire: An Acceptance in the Third Person (Garden City, New York, 1937), make up "The Nightmare." In it, Cabell experiments with Lewis Carroll's technique of the dream-story which obeys "the actual and well-known laws of a normal dream" (Quiet, Please, p. 58). The "Heirs and Assigns" trilogy is comprised of Hamlet Had an Uncle: A Comedy of Honor (New York, 1940), The King Was in His Counting House: A Comedy of Common-Sense (New York, 1938), and The First Gentleman of America: A Comedy of Conquest (New York, 1942). Based on historical sources, the trilogy moves from primitive Scandinavia to Renaissance Italy to new-found America. It is unified by its political and ethical themes. Only partially fiction, the final trilogy, "It Happened in Florida," uses various aspects of the state's geography and history. With

A. J. Hanna, Cabell wrote *The St. Johns: A Parade of Diversities* (New York, 1943), about one of Florida's most historically important rivers. *There Were Two Pirates: A Comedy of Division* (New York, 1946), gives a fictional account of José Gasparilla, St. Augustine's legendary pirate. *The Devil's Own Dear Son: A Comedy of the Fatted Calf* (New York, 1949), is a fantasy of modern, tourist-centered Florida.

Cabell's later essays include *Some of Us: An Essay in Epitaphs* (New York, 1930), and two trilogies: "Their Lives and Letters" (*These Restless Heads* [New York, 1932], *Special Delivery* [New York, 1933], *Ladies and Gentlemen* [New York, 1934]), and "Virginians are Various" (*Let Me Lie* [New York, 1947], *Quiet, Please* [Gainesville, Florida, 1952], *As I Remember It* [New York, 1955]). In these essays, Cabell often discusses his own writing as well as his relations with other novelists of the period. See, for example, Mark Schorer's *Sinclair Lewis: An American Life* (New York, 1961). A volume of correspondence, *Between Friends: Letters of James Branch Cabell and Others*, ed. Padraic Colum and Margaret Freeman Cabell (New York, 1962), contains letters from H. L. Mencken, F. Scott Fitzgerald, and Sinclair Lewis.

For recent studies of Cabell's thought and attitudes, one may consult the series of articles by Raymond Himelick, "Cabell, Shelley, and the 'Incorrigible Flesh,'" *South Atlantic Quarterly*, XLVII (1948), 88-95, "Figures of Cabell," *Modern Fiction Studies*, II (1956-1957), 214-220, and "Cabell and the Modern Temper," South Atlantic Quarterly, LVIII (1959), 176-184. These are general studies, emphasizing Cabell's affinities to Swift, Voltaire, and Shelley. Although he could never praise Cabell wholeheartedly, Edd Winfield Parks, "James Branch Cabell," Southern Renascence: The Literature of the Modern South, ed. Louis Rubin, Jr., and Robert Jacobs (Baltimore, 1953), pp. 251-261, "Cabell's Cream of the Jest," Modern Fiction Studies, II (1956-1957), 68-70, "James Branch Cabell," Mississippi Quarterly, XX (1967), 97-102, emphasizes Cabell's humanism. He sees Cabell as a writer of philosophical romance. Robert Canary, "James Branch Cabell and the Comedy of Skeptical Conservatism," Midcontinent American Studies Journal, VI, i (1965), 52-60, and "Cabell's Dark Comedies," Mississippi Quarterly, XXI (1968), 83-92, discusses Cabell's political attitudes and the complex nature of his treatment of sex. Both are very stimulating essays. In "Cabell and His Critics," The Dilemma of the Southern Writer, ed. Richard K. Meeker (Farmville, Virginia, 1961), pp. 119-142, Dorothy Schlegel discusses the effect of criticism on Cabell's work.

  The recent Cabell Revival began in 1948 with Edward Wagenknecht's "Cabell: A Reconsideration," College English, IX (1948), 238-246, later revised as "James Branch Cabell: The Anatomy of Romanticism," Cavalcade of the American Novel (New York, 1952), pp. 339-353, which gives a summary of Cabell's achievement along with an evaluation. Wagenknecht was followed by Edmund Wilson, whose essay "The James Branch Cabell Case Reopened," first appeared in The New Yorker, XXXII (21 April 1956), 140-168, and was collected in The Bit Between My Teeth: A Literary Chronicle of 1950-1965 (New York, 1965), pp. 291-321. Wilson's essay is a survey of Cabell's work with emphasis on its Southern character and nature. He suggests that "The Nightmare Has Triplets," the dream-trilogy, is among Cabell's best work. Louis Rubin, Jr., No Place on Earth: Ellen Glasgow, James Branch Cabell and Richmond-in-Virginia (Austin, Texas, 1959), pp. 50-81, emphasizes Cabell's role as a regional allegorist. His book may be supplemented by two briefer items: "Two in Richmond: Ellen Glasgow and James Branch Cabell," South: Modern Southern Literature and Its Cultural Setting, ed. Louis Rubin and Robert Jacobs (Garden City, New York, 1961), pp. 115-141, and Richmond as a Literary Capital: An Address (Richmond, 1966). In 1962 appeared two excellent book-length studies, Joe Lee Davis's James Branch Cabell (New York, 1962), and Arvin Wells's Jesting Moses: A Study in Cabellian Comedy (Gainesville, 1962). Although not definitive, Davis's discussion of Cabell's life and works is perhaps the best overall study to appear so far. There is an annotated bibliography. Wells concentrates on "The Biography," and emphasizes the philosophical aspects of Cabellian comedy. Desmond Tarrant's James Branch Cabell: The Dream and the Reality (Norman, Oklahoma, 1967), attempts a large-scale reevaluation. However, his study is marred by multiple errors in documentation and proof-reading. His article, "James Branch Cabell (1879-1958): A Reappraisal," Shenandoah, IX iii (1958), 3-9, suggests some of the major points of his book.

Several essays have appeared which are of biographical importance. Emmett Peter, Jr., "Cabell: The Making of a Rebel," Carolina Quarterly, XIV, ii (1962), 74-81, discusses the scandal at William and Mary, and the murder of John Scott in Richmond. Frank Durham, "Love as a Literary Exercise: Young James Branch Cabell Tries His Wings," Mississippi Quarterly, XVIII (1964-1965), 26-37, investigates Cabell's epistolary love affair with Norvell Harrison. Older essays of value are Eudora Ramsay Richardson's "Richmond and Its Writers," Bookman, LXVIII (1928-1929), 449-453, and Emily Clark, "James Branch Cabell," Innocence Abroad (New York, 1931), pp. 35-52. These discuss Cabell's literary life in Richmond.

A long-time friend of Cabell, Ellen Glasgow, The Woman Within (New York, 1954), pp. 130-136, describes meeting him during his troubled period at William and Mary, while she was researching The Voice of the People. Several critical essays deal jointly with Cabell and Glasgow, among them are Marshall Fishwick's "Cabell and Glasgow: Tradition in Search of Meaning," Shenandoah, VIII, iii (1957), 24-35, and "Two Roads from Eden," Modern Age, II (1957-1958), 404-407, and Nancy Minter McCollum,

"Glasgow's and Cabell's Comedies of Virginia," Georgia Review, XVIII (1964), 236-241. For the latest comment, see Edgar MacDonald, "The Glasgow-Cabell Entente," American Literature, XLI (1969), 76-91.

Although the present bibliography has been an attempt to indicate Cabell's major publications in fiction and belles-lettres, and to suggest some trends in Cabell criticism, many items are not mentioned. The reader interested in a full listing should see Frances Joan Brewer, James Branch Cabell: A Bibliography of His Writings, Biography and Criticism (Charlottesville, Virginia, 1957), and its companion volume, Matthew J. Bruccoli, James Branch Cabell: A Bibliography, Part II: Notes on the Cabell Collections at the University of Virginia (Charlottesville, 1957). Brewer's bibliography has been superceded by James N. Hall and Nelson Bond's James Branch Cabell: A Complete Bibliography (Brooklyn, N.Y.: Revisionist Press, 1975). Two reviews of Cabell scholarship are Joe Lee Davis's "Recent Cabell Criticism," Cabellian, I, i (1968), 1-12, and Edgar E. MacDonald's "Cabell Criticism: Past, Present, and Future," Cabellian, I, i (1968), 21-25.